The Price and Privilege of Growing Old

The Price and Privilege of Growing Old

by W. Gunther Plaut

Illustrated by Roy Doty

CCAR Press · 2000

2009 08 07 06 05 04 03 02 01 2000   10 9 8 7 6 5 4 3 2 1

Library of Congress Cataloging-in-Publication Data

Plaut, W. Gunther. 1912–
    The price and privilege of growing old / by W. Gunther Plaut ;
illustrated by Roy Doty.
      p.   cm.
    ISBN 0-88123-080-4 (hardcover). — ISBN 0-88123-081-2 (pbk.)
    1. Aged—United states—Social conditions. 2. Plaut, W. Gunther,
1912– . 3. Aging—United States. 4. Old age—United States.
5. Retirement—United States. I. Title.
HQ1064.U5P59 1999
305.26'0973—dc21   99-33766
                                                   CIP

DESIGNED BY *Barry Nostradamus Sher*

CCAR Press
355 Lexington Avenue
New York, NY 10017
www.ccarnet.org

Contents

Preface

My father was only sixty-eight years old when, fifty years ago, he died suddenly. Among the many sayings with which he spiced his speech was one that has a direct bearing on this book. He phrased it as a puzzle: "What is it that most people want to become but nobody wants to be?"

Well, what is it? The answer is—old. We'd like to reach old age, but when we get there we find that it is a mixed blessing. It brings with it a diminution of physical powers and often of mental powers as well, and while the decline may be minimal (at least at first), in the long run it spares no one.

Of course we don't expect it to happen the way it does—to others, yes, but not to oneself. I distinctly remember when, as a young man, I dreamt of being immortal. I was mentally alert and physically gifted as an athlete; I would play five sets of tennis in a tournament, then bike home for forty-five minutes and suffer no aches or pains the next day. Exhaustion was something that others experienced, not I. When my brother was born and my maternal grandmother came to celebrate the joyous occasion, I asked her to turn a somersault to express her stated delight. I thought she was unduly stubborn for not doing such a small thing for me and found her excuse that she was too old for such a venture most disappointing. I was six years old at the time. She would often tell the story of my incomprehension, and obviously her refusal made a lasting impression on me.

The six-year-old mindset wore off in the course of time, though very slowly. I am very fortunate in that I can still work and enjoy it, though I am closer to the ninety- than the eighty-year mark. My mind is clear—clear enough anyway to assess my own aging process frankly.

When the media deal with the old they frequently present pictures of people in some dreary setting, staring vacantly into the future. Unfortunately, the picture is real enough, but it does not represent the vast majority of the old. After all, only about eight percent of the senior population inhabit any kind of institution.

This book punctures some myths and highlights the prejudice that society visits on its aged component. It has not been written for the sake of shocking anyone or lessening the enjoyment of life. Quite the contrary. What I am trying to do is to supplement the current barrage of how-to-age tomes with a bit of realism, and do so from the inside, that is, from the perspective of someone who has followed the course of his own aging with close attention. Happily, there's more to it than decline. Like many of my contemporaries, I have experienced aging as a time of serenity, ease of mind, and growth. The marketplace of competition and the urge for acquisition have become memories. The here and now are real, and thoroughly enjoyable. For me and multitudes like me, the price of growing old is more than balanced by the privilege it can bestow.

For those to whom I am a stranger: I was born in Germany, graduated from law school, and, having been thrown out by the Nazis because I was a Jew, migrated to the United States, where I became a rabbi. After nearly forty years in the ministry in the States and in Canada, I changed occupations and turned to full-time writing and lecturing, while continuing my involvement with communal endeavors. My wife and I have been blessed with sixty years of companionship and with children and grandchildren.

I am now learning the ups and downs of aging — its problems and fortunately, also its rewards. This book is about both. Many insights that others have given me are mirrored in its pages, and I hope that my readers will find their own lives enriched by them, as I did.

These pages were written from the perspective of confident realism. In the context of aging that may sound like an oxymoron, but it need not be. I'd like to think that the kind of realism purveyed in this book has confidence and hope built into it and that this will reassure those readers who want to face the prospect of aging and ultimate departure from this world with less anxiety and increased self-understanding. For this purpose I have also assembled a fair amount of information, drawn from many sources and times. The possibilities and problems of aging have been with the human race from the beginning.

The United Nations has proclaimed 1999 the International Year of Older Persons. Let us hope that will mean for both young and old a heightened awareness of the promise that life can hold for all of us.

W. Gunther Plaut

> Old age is an incurable disease.
> *Seneca (died 65 CE)*

> Old age is the only disease
> we don't look forward
> to being cured of.
> *Anonymous*

PRELUDE

Why We Age

All creatures age and do so at various speeds. The shorter their life span the quicker their ability to procreate, the longer their life span the more slowly do they awaken to the need of passing on their genes to the next generation. The way of achieving this goal is almost universally based on a usually cooperative male/female act, called sex, though some species have their own way of achieving the same purpose. Some fish die in the process and a certain female spider consumes her mate after the act, but generally the sexual encounter is not life threatening—on the contrary, for humans it is pleasurable and desirable, even when procreation is not at issue.

Procreation represents nature's answer to death, and death occurs for three reasons: violence, illness, and aging. The latter two are the subject of millennia of speculation and of continued inquiry, while violence is something animals and humans have known about from the beginning of their existence and still have reason to know about, fear, and try to escape.

That leaves illness and aging as the two other causes of our physical destruction, unless aging is itself an illness (using the word in its common sense). Seneca, a Roman writer who lived two thousand years ago, was probably the first to take this view. "Old age," he said, "is an incurable disease." A rabbi took the same line later on and wrote: "Old age is one big sickness, yet all aspire to it."

Since the aging of our cells may indeed be due to an illness, our medical researchers are trying their best to keep this "aging disease" (like any other sickness) from killing us. They have already helped us to live longer — and no one knows at present how far this will stretch human longevity. Keeping one's body going forever is not (or not yet) a common goal, and at this writing and for a long while beyond we will be subject to the fate of Adam and Eve, who were forced to leave the Garden of Eden, lest they would eat the fruit of the Tree of (Eternal) Life.

However, by current scientific standards death is not an illness at all but an ineluctable aspect of life itself, a normal process of deterioration built into the very cells that form the basis of our existence. If that is true, death is simply the other side of life, so that everything living has, literally, a deadline. Just how long one might live is ascribed by most people today to one's genes, a healthy life style, medical progress, and/or the will of God. This conglomeration of contributing causes is part of our contemporary complexities. Formerly it was universally believed that life and death depended primarily on the will of an omnipotent deity or the capriciousness of fate. Greek gods especially were thought to be willful and therefore unpredictable, while a non-capricious but equally unknowable God was perceived by Jews (and later, Christians and Muslims) as willing to listen to people's prayers and responding to pious deeds. Superstitions of countless types and numbers have contributed additional efforts to postpone the inevitable.

Legends too have played their role, telling of certain people falling into a deep sleep and awakening years later to a world sometimes quite strange to them. Thus, the Talmud tells of Rabbi Simeon bar Yochai, who with his son hid in a cave for twelve years to escape from his enemies, a feat made possible by a miracle; and Washington Irving invented Rip Van Winkle, who slept for twenty years. Modern science, through research in the relatively new field of cryonics, has already begun to create real-life versions of Rip by freezing human sperm and other tissues and organs. But if some people hope to be frozen rather than buried, and to be unfrozen at a future date when they can be revived and preserved from further deterioration, they are not likely to meet with success-not yet, anyway. While this new branch of biology can already preserve certain body parts, it is a long way from preserving whole animals and humans. One student of the subject said a generation ago that the complexity of such life systems renders artificial preservation impossible, but there are laboratories at work today that aim to give the lie to this assumption.

An entirely different endeavor aims at rearranging the building blocks of life, through molecular engineering (nanotechnology), which follows a simple logic: if we can take the atoms found in sand and make computer chips of them, what limits are there to rearranging the particles that constitute life and thereby snatching physical immortality from the jaws of time? For the time being, ordinary folk continue to believe that life is ultimately limited, but just how limited is being constantly put to the test.

There is also the Genome Project, that is, the identification and analysis of all genes in the human body (estimated at some three billion bases). When that project is finished-possibly early in the 21st century-and the genes for the major contributors to the various factors that produce aging are located and mapped, experiments with induced mutations will be commonplace. The kind of aging we experience today will potentially be different and postponed and even the certainty of death will be scientifically questioned. Those who support this kind of vision have been dubbed "immortalists." They believe that in time we will be able to fix this or that part of the body that contributes to aging, replace it if necessary, and thus prolong life indefinitely. We may have a new heart, new kidneys, or whatever, maybe even a new brain. We'll be like an automobile that in the course of time has every part replaced and functions as if new. Taking this thought to its extreme, we would in effect have so many parts changed that we end up as someone else. Aging might disappear, but so might we, with our particular identities.

Quite recently, a new contender in the race for immortality has emerged. Already in the early sixties, biologist Leonard Hayflick concluded that the ordinary human cell divides about fifty times before it quits its self-renewal. By preventing the enzyme telomerase from shortening the tails of chromosomes (called telomeres), the so-called Hayflick Limit of divisions has been doubled in laboratory studies, suggesting to some observers that we may eventually look to a vastly extended life span. But the subject of cell division is extraordinarily complicated, for cancer, the old enemy of health and aging, is the champion when it comes to cell division and has already defied the Hayflick limit. The telomeres of cancer cells do not shorten, permitting uncontrolled cell division. Nonetheless, the consensus among the biologists seems to be that we are at the portal of influencing longevity in a radical manner.

Research into the behavior of collagen goes in the same direction and is also occupied with cell division. Collagen is a common fibrous protein in our bodies and may be described as providing the essential structure of the human body, since it is the major component of skin and bones, teeth and cartilage, blood vessels, ligaments and tendons. Healthy collagen replaces itsself regularly, and lack of such replacement may be identical with aging. Brain cells do not generally keep on dividing, yet their protein components are being replaced constantly, and when that process slows, the brain (and we with it) may be said to be aging. And lately, a Toronto scientist has led a team of researchers in identifying the capacities of the PTEN gene to override the normal life-and-death cycle of the cell. Injecting a moribund cell with a virus carrying PTEN restored the cell to normalcy. Journalists were quick to hail this not only as a breakthrough but also as a new window on immortality.

All of which adds up to this: There is no single cause of aging but a complex interplay of cellular changes that amount to a process of deterioration and eventual malfunctioning. For instance, tiny amounts of calcium accumulate in the valves and muscles of the heart, and in consequence a yellow-brown pigment called lipofuscin is deposited in its tissues, a process called "browning" (when I first read of it I thought of an apple which browns when cut open and is exposed to oxygen). How science will help us manage these changes remains to be seen, but that it will succeed on some levels seems likely. There are other processes that appear to contribute (though not always) to the complexity of what constitutes aging, such as high metabolic rate, high blood sugar, high body temperature, and even amount of food consumed (it seems that less is better). Strange as it may seem, birds have become a major focus of gerontological research, for many of them have significant longevity, even though they face conditions that, in humans, would be highly damaging:

> Birds, for instance, may be exposed to five times as much oxygen per cell as humans during a lifetime. The same is true of browning, which should be a much more serious problem for birds, with their high blood sugar and body temperature, than for humans.
>
> But given bird longevity, it apparently isn't. What protection have they evolved that we haven't? . . . We should be in a position before too many more years to begin putting bird antibrowning or antioxidation genes into mice, for instance, to duplicate the cellular damage resistance that birds possess. If our current theories about aging are accurate, this should represent a big step toward the 10-year mouse, and perhaps the 150-year human, life span.

Maybe. Such high human ages would put enormous stress on the capacity of the earth to feed us and provide a livable climate, quite aside from the fundamental changes they would impose on the structure of human societies. For the time being, the proverbial saying that "nothing is certain but death and taxes" still reflects a basic fact of human existence. Gerontologist Steven Austad puts it this way:

> Aging is a consequence of normal biological processes that nature designed for our benefit, but which also possess inescapable and damaging side effects or inherent dangers. Aging is a product of our genes, because our genes direct and carry out these processes.

Maybe radical scientific breakthroughs are around the corner, in which case this book will be filed under "Primitive Antiquity" which will describe the time when people actually died, or died young, at 100. There is even today a Journal of Anti-Aging Medicine, though its editor, Dr. Michael Fossel, has warned that scientists might just achieve what people seem to ask for, in which case everything we know will be changed-from family to economy to everything else. Similarly, Sherwin B. Nuland, a thoughtful student of these issues, cautions us:

Mankind cannot afford to destroy the balance by tinkering with one of its most essential elements, which is the constant renewal within individual species and the invigoration that accompanies it. This is what is meant by the cycles of nature. To thwart it is the first step toward thwarting the continuation of exactly that which we try to preserve, which is, after all, the order and system of the universe.

Meanwhile, however, we are like other species: stuck with being mortal. Getting old compares to a train riding the rails to the terminal. Yet, though we become chronologically older and approach our destination, we are not considered old as long as our Western society continues on its present course of downplaying and, subconsciously, denying human mortality.

I should add that all the above-noted efforts to prolong human life mean little to that element of society that doesn't want to wait for usable results. Thus, human growth hormone (HGH) helps people grow muscles where there were none to speak of, and while there seem to be dangers lurking, people who desire magic results will likely take their chances — if they can afford it. They will quote the Internet advice dished out by some doctor who advises to "grow young with HGH":

> If you are already suffering the ill effects of aging, you could turn the clock back 20 years and stay that way until the century mark. . . . The right amount of it at the right time promises to bring about the most fundamental revolution in society today, the beginning of the end of aging.

The reporter adds: "The [web] sites sound as if they are selling eternity. That could be what the consumer gets."

PART ONE

LOOKING AT MYSELF

When I Became Tired and Retired

My Threshold of Change

I never thought it would happen to me, but it did. It's natural for a teenager, tasting the first glories of life, to believe that physical mortality is something that befalls others only. I must have remained a teenager for many years, for my *joie de vivre* and physical stamina seemed inexhaustible. Fatigue was a condition that even in my fifties I experienced only now and then. My work day started at 5:30 in the morning and lasted into the night. It took a while for my body to be satisfied with six hours' sleep, but then it became routine.

For me, the first sign of aging surfaced when I was in my early sixties, and I can still recall the shock it produced. I was a congregational rabbi at the time, which meant I was on call seven days a week, all hours of the day and occasionally at night as well. I had already learned early on that for rabbis (as for ministers and priests), the religious rest day is for others, but is a workday for them-they are required to fulfill often arduous duties on that very day. These are rewarding, to be sure, but teaching, conducting services, and preaching, as well as meeting congregants *en masse* and individually, are fatiguing, however satisfying.

At Holy Blossom, a synagogue with over two thousand member families, my daily responsibilities were literally endless. In addition to meeting congregational tasks, I was active in the wider community, both Jewish and general; I served as a member of national and international boards, which required a fair amount of travel; I was a regular columnist for Canada's *Globe & Mail* and had other literary deadlines to meet. My wife, Elizabeth, was becoming engaged in her own pursuits in the field of genealogy, and our children were grown up by then.

A rabbi's major "season" winds down as spring ends and the heavy stone of fatigue rolls off the rabbinic chest. For work during the summer is relatively easy and provides time for taking a deep breath, for a vacation, for physical and mental restoration. Since I first entered the ministry in 1939, and with the exception of my years in the army, this had been my experience. And that's when it happened.

The spring festival of Shavuot (Pentecost) had passed, and the anticipation of leisure was beckoning. Except this time, I felt none of the relief I had hoped for. Instead of becoming carefree I was suddenly wondering how, come fall, I would handle the work load. Rather than feeling liberated I felt depressed—not clinically, but enough to worry me. Obviously something had changed. The first signs of aging had set in, and I became aware of it on that spring day in 1976. I was not quite 64 years old.

I shared my feelings with Elizabeth, and that summer we talked about it off and on. I could do nothing about getting older; I could, however, do something about my job. I was doing too much, and the more I did the more was expected of me. Counseling was becoming a burden. People had to wait weeks before they could get an appointment, and when they finally came, at four-thirty or five o'clock in the afternoon, I was fatigued and less than fully attentive to their needs and hopes. The half-hour counseling session was too short for them and too long for me. I had already felt for some time that I was being less than fair to people who looked to me for help, and I had blamed my work schedule for my fatigue. Now it occurred to me that maybe my advancing years had something to do with it, and I wondered how to manage my future. Clearly, I had suffered from professional burnout, though at the time I did not call it by that name. (Maybe I should have taken to heart the biblical precedent, which rules that those serving in the ancient Tabernacle must retire at 50.)

It happened that another aspect of my daily labors tipped the scales of decision. Since 1964 I had been working on my life's major scholarly enterprise, a commentary on the Torah (the Five Books of Moses). I was to write part of it and edit the whole. I had published the first volume to much public acclaim, and the rest of the project was well looked after—at least so it appeared. But serious setbacks occurred: the Board of Advisors that oversaw the publication turned one author's manuscript back, another indicated he could not proceed, and then—after I had personally assumed their assignments—lightning struck. The rabbinic scholar (a close friend of ours) who had begun labors on the last of the five books died suddenly. The whole enterprise threatened to grind to a halt, just when my own life had entered a difficult period. The work I considered the major goal of my literary and scholarly efforts was in danger of disappearing below the horizon of my hopes.

I asked my congregation to consider engaging a co-rabbi, and offered to contribute half my salary in order to make this possible. But the leadership worried that such an arrangement would not work. Two heads on one body would be a recipe for trouble, they said, and pointed to some unhappy precedents. My proposal went nowhere.

That solution having failed, a difficult choice lay before me: I could continue as a congregational rabbi and abandon the Torah project or retire and devote myself entirely to its completion. Apparently I could not have it both ways.

My wife and I explored the choices at great length: what it would mean to us as a family (my mother was greatly afraid of the change), how it would affect our finances, and the like. We finally concluded that completing the Torah commentary was more important than completing another few years as rabbi of Holy Blossom, though it was by general consensus one of the best posts of its kind anywhere. Once the decision was made, we were greatly relieved and knew instinctively that we had done the right thing. The congregation was generous and made the transition as easy as it could, even continuing my employment on a minimal scale.

When the burdens of responsibility were lifted, I felt as if youth were paying me another visit. However, the visit was of limited duration, though it was nice while it lasted. I had passed the first threshold of aging.

I Forgot Her Name

If my first indicator of aging was general fatigue, the second was confined to the mind. I had always been good at remembering people's names, and my job as a rabbi helped me to stay keen. All members of the clergy know that people are pleased when they are called by name, their identity thus being acknowledged and affirmed by their religious leader. They are known as individuals, not merely an anonymous part of the crowd. Long practice in the rabbinate had enhanced my memory, and maybe my Old World schooling, with its endless assignments of memorizing this or that, plus years of playing chess (doing it blindfolded on occasion), had sharpened whatever helps to recall someone's name.

In fact, at times I became quite cocky about this capacity, and I occasionally played a memory game with people. When I lectured in some city, my schedule usually included an informal discussion in someone's home. Rarely were more than twenty-five people present, and when I was introduced to them one at a time I would concentrate on their names and some distinctive features like their clothing, for memory goes with association of one form or another. It is not as difficult as it sounds. When the evening's discussion started I would address a questioner by name, and when I continued doing it with one or two others there would be general astonishment, which greatly helped the cause I was promoting and made me more credible. For me, it was a game, and no one got hurt. But then one evening I didn't seem to get the hang of it. I wondered why I could not manage it, and never tried it again. The moment you start doubting yourself, it doesn't work.

But that was only the start. Back home, at a congregational gathering, I saw a woman approaching me whom I recognized as a long-time acquaintance. Suddenly I realized that I could not remember her name, and though I managed to survive the impasse without embarrassment I was perturbed and felt quite insecure. That first experience with a "senior moment" was repeated now and then, and I knew that another stage of aging had been reached. My friends told me that they had been forgetting names for quite some time, and it now became painfully clear that this particular deterioration had not passed me by.

It seemed to me that forgetting names was different from other types of memory failure, for it appears to be the first mental contraction and is in fact a universal experience. When I discussed this with a gerontologist and asked why this was so, he told me that name retrieval constituted a fairly new area of intensive investigation. There is now a magazine, called *Memory*, devoted to a special inquiry into "prosopamnesia" (also "proper name amnesia"). The current theory suggests that in a way the brain acts like a computer in that it stores information in various files and various ways. Names are kept, so to speak, in a special file in the frontal lobe of the brain. As we age, this storage place appears to be the first memory file affected. Since the thousands of different items it contains are quite diverse and lack association, they are difficult to call up. The more we can link items we want to remember to a context or other memories, the easier it is be to transfer them to our conscious mind. Retrieval of names (not only those of people) is thus a kind of discontinuous enterprise that will occasionally threaten us with failure.

But why should age become a factor? Dr. Gordon Winocur, who specializes in memory research at Toronto's Baycrest Centre for Geriatric Care, says that in fact we older people who are otherwise healthy suffer a surprisingly small memory loss. When a significant loss does occur, we are likely to find that some decline in our general physical capacity has taken place, for health factors have a more severe impact on us as we age. There are other reasons too: Certain drugs or combinations of drugs may impair memory. Our circadian (24 hour) rhythm also plays a role, for we are alert at certain times and inattentive at others. Furthermore, Dr. Winocur emphasizes, the aged are usually stereotyped by society as a forgetful bunch, and when we hear this often enough it may become a self-fulfilling prophecy. If we start believing that forgetting is natural for us, our ability to remember will likely weaken Finally, it is good to know that "implicit memory," which relates to the skills we have already learned, usually suffers no loss at all. We don't forget how to swim, ride a bike, or drive a car, though we will certainly need practice to continue doing it well. In most instances this is also true for knowledge we have acquired and assimilated: A good chess player will continue to play the game well; a seasoned cook will remember great recipes; and aged scholars will be able to call up the essentials of their specialty.

Occasional events that don't matter much to us will soon be forgotten, and not by the old alone. The more specific and the more interesting the event, the more likely it will stick with us. Dr. Winocur gives this example: Driving through a rural area, you notice some black dots in a field. The eyes take it in for a split second, but memory does not. If, however, you discover that the dots are in fact cows, memory may begin to pay attention, and if you are familiar with breeds and recognize the animals as Angus cattle you probably will remember the "black dots" quite readily.

Familiarity also helps memory. For this reason, the private rooms of residents in the new Jewish Home for the Aged in Toronto are being built large enough to accommodate some of the residents' furniture and other familiar things, to assist them to see the past more clearly and remember it more vividly.

It is not inappropriate to think of the brain as resembling a muscle, which deteriorates if it is not used enough. When I ceased being a congregational rabbi and no longer met crowds of people whom I had to know by name, my memory brain-file for names started malfunctioning more frequently. Fortunately, it has not worsened too badly, though lately I have also encountered an occasional blockage in word retrieval during a public speech. Most of the time I speak without a manuscript, and once in a while the exact term I am looking for is hiding from me and I have to resort to circumlocution and thereby hide the problem. Meanwhile, I am aware that aging gives me all sorts of signals.

As noted above, in the public mind memory loss is believed to be quite regularly associated with aging. But except for particular illnesses such as Alzheimer's or some other form of dementia, being old does not make one automatically prone to forget what happened ten minutes ago or yesterday. In fact, while we may experience some forgetfulness, memory and other brain functions usually hold up better than other physiological capacities. Then again, in our society aging has become increasingly stressful in hidden or obvious ways, and stress has been identified in recent studies as producing certain steroids that damage the synapses (the gateways for nerve impulses) in the hippocampus, which controls our memory. We do not know whether this was also the case in times when the aged were revered as custodians of tradition—another aspect of being old that awaits discovery.

There's also a general perception that aging folk lack flexibility or are for whatever reason incapable of learning new things. Nonsense. My mother started university at age 88 and so did a friend of hers—in fact, the two seemed to compete with one another—and what they did demonstrated clearly the enduring capacity to learn. (As many readers may remember, Mother receiving her B.A. at one hundred was given wide publicity.) Elizabeth and I were in our seventies when we began writing on computers, and both she and I have published books since then. Still, one hears people say, "You can't teach an old dog new tricks." Nonsense again—literally. We had a canine companion who at age 12 (equivalent to being 80+ in human terms) became blind. It took him very little time to accustom himself to his new condition. One day we installed in our home an accordion door in a previously open passageway and had to acquaint him with the new barrier. We were sure that he would be incapable of opening it, for it was the first such contraption for him as for us. Surprise! He got up on his hind legs, experimented with the latch, learned that the door opened by folding rather than swinging, and had it down pat in no time at all. For people too, if they are healthy, learning at any age is primarily a matter of will, and it becomes easier by habituation.

Retirement Redefines Us

There are some things between heaven and earth that the retired have not heard or thought about.

The first thing they are likely to discover is that they have lost an important part of their identity and suddenly have to explain who they are, which is something they never anticipated. When they meet someone they don't know, the first thing they will be asked is, "What do you do?" How are they to respond? Among the answers I often hear are these:

"What do I do? Nothing!"

"You want to know the truth? I'm bored."

"I'm retired, but frankly, I'm more tired than retired" (a pun that sidesteps a meaningful response).

"I'm busy looking after my investments" (I have heard this response from a few, but was not sure whether it was a cover for doing little or nothing).

"I do what I want to do and not what I have to do, and I enjoy every moment of my freedom." (I like that the best, and in its general thrust it describes where I find myself.)

After a while retirees get used to giving a "proper" answer to the query, one that fits their needs and self-esteem. My private and totally unscientific survey shows that the most popular response is, "What do I do? You wouldn't believe it, I'm busier than I ever was!"

Being busy becomes a task in itself. There are those who spend their time volunteering, but I have found them to be in the minority. There are the affluent who spend part of their time traveling, reveling in sunny climes, or move to sun cities altogether, where leisure activities are carefully and amply programmed.

Time-filling activities abound. There are the golfers, skiers, bridge or other card aficionados — while readers of books, like sun worshippers, seem to be decreasing in numbers. Still others are those who take courses of one kind or another; learn to play an instrument, paint, or sculpt — the choices are many and I have no knowledge of any statistics that would quantify them.

The fact is that everyone is doing one thing or another, and for all I know most of them are enjoying their leisure time. But the focus provided by paid work is gone, and because of that, retirees have to refashion their self-image and their waking hours. I'm aware that I have gathered my information primarily from men, though not entirely so. The women I have asked tend to revert to an old-fashioned perspective and say something like this: "Thank God I can spend more time with family and friends than I ever could." All have to grapple with the image problem, and as always in life, some do it more successfully than others. But all of them share one thing, though they hesitate to face it: While work gave them identity in the past, they have now been officially declared obsolete by our culture (more of which later).

I could fool the reader and state that the identity problem did not concern me, because people who knew me at all knew of some of my activities. Still, I too lost some of my identity when I ceased being the rabbi of a great congregation. I found out, for instance, that I was after a while discontinued from some boards on which I had enjoyed serving. Younger people were needed to bring new ideas to the board, I was told. Just when I had more time for them, they had other plans for me. Since these changes did not happen all at once, they did not cause me any serious disappointment—nothing lasts forever, I told myself. But after a while I got the idea: In the past my value had often been my presence rather than my potential contribution, because the boardroom culture required people like me with certain job titles. It was in a way like visiting sick people in their hospital rooms: They wanted me there as the rabbi of the Temple, and less so for whatever comfort I would provide or prayer I might offer. When people had greeted me on occasion by saying, "I'm so honored you came," my wife had often reminded me: "Don't let it go to your head, it's the office that honors them, not you." She was right, and retirement only underlined the truth of it. The whole identity shift didn't happen all at once; it just built up (or rather down) with a kind of slow inevitability.

While I still do some work for the congregation, it might appear in retrospect as if my retreat from full-time employment was proof that age 65 is indeed a physiological watershed for people, quite aside from cultural custom. But I now think it was nothing of the kind. I wanted to do other work primarily and had no desire to check out from working altogether. It turned out, in fact, that my most creative years were still ahead of me. I was getting old, all right, and had passed an important threshold of my life. But if the rabbinate had been my only occupation I would not have changed my work, and no one would have required it of me. It had been my decision. I was one person trying to rearrange his existence more wisely, but unfortunately most people don't have the luxury of individual choice.

In Canada we're obsolete by fiat at age sixty-five in the majority of government positions, even in such unlikely places as universities. Yet at that time of life the average professor is probably at the height of her or his mental capacity and has accumulated experience to make the most of it. Judges have a ten-year leeway, and so do senators (who are appointed). In the United States, the FDR-introduced social security age is now under fire and already abandoned in some instances, but it remains the critical finish line for the moment. Demographically, that moment has overstayed its welcome, for sixty-five no longer has any significance on the longevity curve.

Even physiologically, those aged sixty-five are today what fifty-five or even fifty-year old people used to be. Retirement in the old sense is fast becoming obsolete. A lot of people at sixty-five need to work at least part-time, and not just for economic reasons. Marrying late is merely an indicator of the age shift that has already taken place. Middle age used to be heralded by one's fortieth birthday. It has advanced a whole ten years, and will keep on doing so for the foreseeable future. The old chronology of aging has become meaningless.

Admittedly, for a long time the current retirement system has been an economic blessing for the majority of working families, though they had to come to terms with the loss of identity they suffered when they said good-bye to their daily pilgrimage to office or factory. The separation of long-term employees formerly was (and often still is) attended by some sort of ceremony, highlighted by the presentation of a token gift, maybe the proverbial gold watch. I sometimes think of the watch as a metaphor that describes what happens to us when we are decommissioned. Its basic function is its capacity to tell time accurately, and its gold cover has little to do with that. When I was retired from the Army of the United States in 1946, I was allowed to keep the steel watch I had been issued. I am happy to report that it proves the usefulness of things old, for it is still performing well when I wind it, though I do so rarely in these days of battery-driven horologes. A lot of retired folk would like to be valued not for having reached the "golden age" but for who they are and what they can still contribute. Lots of them keep excellent time when given a chance.

Mirror, Mirror on the Wall

About the time of my retirement from congregational work, my mother (then 85 years old) said to me, "I don't like the way your face looks. It has changed." We joked about it, of course, but when I got home I took a good look at myself in the mirror. Mutti, as I and many others called her, was right. My features seemed to have become more angular; my long face appeared longer, my cheek bones more pronounced. It must have happened over some period, but I hadn't noticed it. The smooth, even contours were going or already gone. Our faces serve as the visiting cards we present to the world, and suddenly my card had an additional inscription: "Aging Man."

Memories of my erstwhile dream of immortality flickered before my eyes, but that did nothing to alter my visage.

Since I could do nothing about my image, my subconscious gave me the kind of advice that, I found out later, others have followed also: "Don't admire yourself in the mirror." Henceforth I stopped all attempts of self-admiration and looked only for what I needed to see, as for instance whether my hair (what was left of it) could pass a cursory inspection.

For a while I shaved in semi-darkness to lessen my displeasure at seeing myself, and when I looked I focused on the spot where the razor was supposed to go, not on my face as a whole. But in time I got used to reality, more or less anyway.

So, how can others whose circumstances are very different from mine tell when old age has sneaked up on them? Public wit responds: When the doctor, and not the police, tell you to slow down. There are other, and less threatening markers. For instance:

You're in the bus or subway, and a courteous younger person gets up for you and offers you her or his seat. When a thirty-year old stood up for me — the first time it happened — I was a bit shocked. Today I would welcome the gesture.

Or watch for a simple remark that will tell the tale unmistakably. Someone meets you who has not seen you for a while, and wants to pay you a compliment. You may hear a pleasant-sounding hello like this: "My, you look well!" or something like it. Then you know you have passed the magic barrier, for your acquaintance would never dream of saying it to a younger person. When it is said to me I respond with as much grace as the moment permits, and often the following brief dialogue takes place:

"My, you look well!"

"Thanks, that's because I'm in my third age."

" Really?! How's that?"

"That's because human life is divided into three ages."

"And what are they?"

"Youth, middle age, and 'you look well.'"

The response usually evokes laughter, because I seem to have responded to a pleasant greeting with something that sounds like clever repartee. Actually, when someone tells me how well I look I am indeed pleased. For a lot of people know my chronological age, and a kind remark is appreciated. The worm has turned: Whereas formerly I was put off a bit, now I wait for the compliment. The years roll by and leave their mark.

Women might hear a variation: "You look more beautiful than ever." Chalk that one up to grace (the speaker's) and aging (your own).

Guilt has no feet, but it surely has a way of getting to you quickly

It's not easy to be a parent, and it's not easy to be a child.

Of Marriage, Sandwiches & Other Things

The Best and Worst Day

Writing frankly about my marriage of sixty years is not meant to instruct the reader; this is not a treatise on how to manage marital affairs. It is simply one person's assessment of how the years have dealt and are dealing with him and his life's companion, now that we reached the latter years of life. Others may contemplate their own existence and in the contrast or likeness find cause for taking a good look at themselves.

Charles Dickens started *A Tale of Two Cities* by describing the book's setting as both the best and worst of times. In a way, my wedding day turned out to be like that.

I had arrived penniless in America, in the midst of the Great Depression, and was still a student at Hebrew Union College in Cincinnati when I met Elizabeth. It was April 1938, and in November we were married. "Why wait?" we thought. We were both in our late twenties, rather tardy for marriage in those days.

After the wedding, we found out that while we were celebrating, over a thousand synagogues and prayer places in Germany had been burned or vandalized by the Nazis; countless Jews had been arbitrarily arrested, killed or sent to concentration camps; and my own father had escaped this fate only because a kindly police constable had tipped him off, allowing him to go into hiding for several weeks. Except for my younger brother, no one of my family was present at my wedding, held on *Kristallnacht,* the pogrom night that, as we were to learn later, was the beginning of the Holocaust. Thenceforth it was open season on Jews.

I don't know how an odds-maker would have rated our chances for marital success, but it did not occur to us to ask and we blissfully charged ahead. Were we well matched? At first glimpse, no. A *shadchan* (professional arranger of marriages) might not have chosen us as a likely couple. We were both still in school. Elizabeth was a scientist/teacher in training; I was educated in law (in Germany) and hoped to be ordained as a rabbi the following spring.

She had been brought up in the security of America; I had been robbed of my career and was scarred by having endured two and a half years of Hitler's madness.

She belonged to a well established family that had been in the States for well over a hundred years; I was a greenhorn who had come to America as a refugee student three years before, and I was poor.

Hers had been a world of women, for her father had died when she was two years old, and she had been raised by her mother, with a grandmother in the house; I was privileged to have grown up with both parents, with Dad being my admired intellectual mentor.

Elizabeth was sociable by nature and modest about her significant scholarly achievements; I was somewhat of a loner, highly insecure and not a little conceited, though today I haven't the foggiest notion about what.

She was a first-rate swimmer and had a life-saving certificate; I could hardly keep afloat but was a passionate athlete otherwise and was highly competitive—which she was not.

For her, music was as essential as breathing; she was totally familiar with the classics and in love with jazz. Her mother was a superb singer and had once been offered a contract from the Metropolitan Opera in New York (an offer she had turned down). I had never been exposed to music, though a piano had graced my family's apartment, for Mother was musical and had a good voice. However, she rarely sang or sat down to play, because Dad disliked music thoroughly, and claimed it hurt his ears.

With all these differences in background, experience, talent, and temperament, what was our common ground?

The ethics we were taught in our homes were identical; yes was yes and not maybe. A promise was made to be kept, not broken. Punctuality was deemed essential, for it was considered an aspect of respect for others. People were valued by who they were and by their background, not by their financial potency. Family background was deemed important. Both of us had been raised in a liberal religious environment, combining faith and tradition with personal choice. Both of us had been brought up to go to the synagogue every Sabbath.

Elizabeth's mother asked a friend who was on his way to Germany to inquire about the reputation of my parents, who did the same in reverse. (Both sides were satisfied.)

Neither of us craved earthly goods; we were both frugal (she by choice and I perforce), and this frugality concerning our personal wants has continued to characterize our household until this day. We both believed that charity and communal service are religious obligations. We have passionately despised discrimination and stereotyping in any form or fashion. We loved books and the arts, and in time, even music became a fertile plot of our common ground. For when Elizabeth took me, a musical ignoramus, to concerts, the Muse soon became a constant guest in our home.

The commonality of our characters and interests easily outweighed our dissimilarities, and many of the latter proved in their very diversity to make our relationship into a richer, multicolored fabric. We were in love, and the years have added mutual respect to make it permanent.

Every marriage is shot through with sacrifice, difficulty, and challenge. In those days, independent careers were rare for married women, and Elizabeth was no exception. She gave up her scientific plans and became the wife of a cleric, a tough, difficult job that engendered a good deal of loneliness for her. When I was shipped overseas to serve in the infantry during World War II, she had to raise our boy alone and was expecting our second child. But a terrible surprise awaited her when the time of delivery arrived: the baby was still-born—a devastating blow at any time, but infinitely more so for Elizabeth, with her husband far away at the German front. The stillbirth was her testing ground, even as the war was mine. I know she had the harder challenge, for she was a war widow (one of the few in her circle), while I was a soldier surrounded by comrades, all sharing the same fate. I'd like to think that because our religious upbringings had made us optimists, we both instinctively looked for the ray of hope in our deep disappointment.

Total trust in one another became the frame of our life. Thus, we always had a joint bank account and considered an "allowance" to be a confirmation of male dominance and therefore demeaning. Without submerging our individual requirements, we learned to think first in terms of "What do *we* need?"

Marital fidelity was a given for us. I for one have found that the steadiness of our relationship did not engender boredom and stifled whatever need I might have developed for sexual diversions. While I admired attractive women and do so to this day, that's as far as it has ever gone. Like everything else in life, feelings too change, and our love of sixty years ago has become a deep-seated affection, of which we speak often and happily. And still, we remain in many ways just as different as we were when we first met.

A large body of literature exists that explores the impact of initial sexual and other expectations on the longevity of marriage. One theory holds that couples who believe that they are destined for each other have a good chance of staying together—but only if their early married days bear out their anticipation. If not, they are said to be the first to seek a divorce. It further appears that one additional and intriguing aspect has to be factored into the equation: successful relationships are enhanced by the resolution, rather than the absence of risks, challenges, and difficulties.

We have learned that living together for a long time does not provide a license for taking each other for granted. The rose garden that has been ours still needs constant watering. This perspective, like everything else in our relationship, became a comfortable and enlarging habit. Last but not least, our children and grandchildren have been the joyful exclamation points of our wedlock. We are a small family, but make up for it by constant attention and mutual affection.

What? No Sex?

Prurient readers may expect that I will go on to describe how aging has affected my sexual interest and performance. Let me quickly say that there are areas of my life that are private and not subject to public inspection, and so my answer will be a loud silence. There are plenty of books on the subject that warn, encourage, give advice, and the like. Swedish researchers are said to have concluded that sexually active older folk have better memories and are generally healthier than those who have given up sex. Those who quit, says the writer, do so more for psychological than for physiological reasons.

There is at least one institution for the aged that I know of that acknowledges the legitimacy of sexual contact in its rules and regulations. The Hebrew Home for the Aged in Riverdale, N.Y., says in its policy preface: "The resident's rights respect the importance of emotional and physical intimacy." It goes on to speak of the "right to seek out and engage in sexual expressions . . . which appear motivated by the desire for sexual gratification," it being understood that the "reasonable sensibilities" of other residents are to be respected as well. The Home was for many years guided by Jacob Reingold, who first proposed the institution of a national Grandparents Day in the U.S.

But unquestionably, there is a residue of unease in a lot of otherwise enlightened folk who raise their eyebrows when they hear of oldsters "fooling around." Maybe that unease rests on a fundamental cultural assumption: The taboos that prohibit intergenerational sexual contacts and specify proper sexual behavior at each stage of the life cycle help regulate the social clock and maintain the full sequence: sex, marriage, work, children. Traditional social norms accept as genuine only the sexuality that is expressed in this sequence. But sex outside these norms continues in the private lives of individuals.

The marriage between Charlie Chaplin and Oona O'Neill certainly passed the sequential test. Their large discrepancy in age was balanced by the large number of children they brought into the world.

The Unwelcome Visitor

Did everything always go smoothly with us? Of course not; we have had our disappointments, especially our inability to have more than two children. We have experienced disagreements, annoyances, and other upsets, but they were temporary and both of us knew it. We have had our operations and bothersome ailments, some of which seem to stick to us like glue. Our knees have gone on unscheduled vacations from their assignments, and I now wear a brace when exercising or going for a long walk. Arthritis encouraged us to give up the house in which we had lived for thirty-four years and, besides, the stairs (like the repair bills) seemed to get steeper with every passing year.

Thus, illness has not passed us by; it has become an expected but unwelcome visitor and has brought worry in its train. We feel we have been warned that what we are doing today we will not always be able to do. There have been changes: Elizabeth's mobility has decreased, and having found out that keeping one's balance cannot be taken for granted, she now uses a cane and occasionally a walker. She has given up driving and I have learned the fundamentals of shopping for groceries and of studying the caloric and fatty content of packaged food—if the print isn't too small. We know that somewhere down the road our physical capacities will be further diminished. I still drive regularly, but am glad to accept a ride for larger distances, when offered.

We still go together on longer trips and attend occasional conventions, while I usually travel alone when fulfilling my lecture engagements. Though such absences are brief, leaving my wife at home casts a shadow over my journeys. Fate has treated us differently in this respect. But while the roles we played in handling our common tasks have changed, the fundamentals of our marital relationship have remained the same. Both of us try to contribute our share to meet each other's needs and at the same time pursue our own individual goals.

Even before we were faced with these new exigencies, we had drawn up living wills. They instruct spouse and doctor not to institute heroic measures for prolonging life when reasonable recovery is no longer attainable. I often wonder what will happen when one of us dies, but this is one subject that Elizabeth does not care to discuss. She is the practical partner, concentrating on going on with life and saying, "Why borrow trouble?" I am given to a more abstract vision of existence, which considers death as a certainty that must be confronted and dealt with, beyond writing testaments and arranging for a burial plot.

In sum, we have been very fortunate. We love our apartment, located at the edge of one of Toronto's ravines, and enjoy the spectacular view, the elevators, and the service rendered by the building staff. We work on our different literary projects in adjoining rooms, yet we have always known that we own no mortgage on the future. For me, growing old has heightened my awareness that the Great Descent has already begun for us. I just don't know when it will gather irreversible speed and leave one of us with the pain of loneliness. Here too life will exact its price: The greater the love, the greater the pain when the beloved is gone. It is a balance we cannot always appreciate.

Of Sandwiches and Care Givers

My father died when he was only 68 years old; my mother lived to nearly 103. Both left me with indelible memories, and both shaped my life far beyond my youth.

The older I become, the more often I seem to quote my late father, although it is now fifty years since he died. Together with his six siblings, he had been raised in a tiny German village and a cramped little house that had been built in 1783. He had no money, became a middle school teacher, and, while he had limited professional ambition, possessed an unlimited thirst for intellectual exploration. His speech was laced with quotations and literary references, and the focal point of our apartment in Berlin was a large library that I was encouraged to use as often as possible. He loved to tell funny stories and crowned them with infectious laughter. He had an uncanny way of giving me sound advice without forcing it on me; in fact, force of any kind was anathema to him, for despite his stern appearance he was a total softy. In England, where Dad and Mother fled in early 1939, he was interned on the Isle of Man because he, the refugee Jew, was now considered a German and therefore an enemy alien. To Dad, who spoke almost no English, this was the ultimate irony—still, he never harbored any grudge against the British, whom he respected for their good manners and love of democracy. When finally, toward the end of the war, my endless petitions for my parents' admission to the United States were approved and they came to the United States, Dad's life was suddenly cut short. A massive heart attack felled him before he had a chance to relish the promise of Minnesota, where we had just moved and where he might have thoroughly enjoyed himself.

Since my childhood I had called him Vati and my mother Mutti, diminutives of *Vater* (father) and *Mutter* (mother), and I continued to do so until they died. No one else, save my brother, would ever have dreamt of addressing Dad as "Vati," but somehow, both in the U.S. and then in Canada, Mother was generally referred to and addressed as "Mutti" by all who felt close to her. It reflected something of the admiration and affection that Dad, with his austere comportment, never seemed to elicit.

Mutti did not have her husband's intellectual acumen, but she had more curiosity, push, and daring—and she was street smart, which he definitely was not. Until she moved with us to Toronto, when she was 71 years old, she had worked most of her life. She then turned full-time to volunteer activity and eventually, at the age of 88, started going to university. She was awarded her B.A. at 100, thereby probably setting a world record. I have described her tale in some detail in a recent book and will not repeat it here. Often I am told that I may have inherited her genes for longevity, and I'll find out soon enough, for time has a way of hurrying on when one becomes old. Our children had already grown up when caring for an aging parent became our responsibility. We thus escaped being dubbed members of the "sandwich generation."

That was just as well, for in any case I am not crazy about that term. It implies that caring for both children and parents puts the middle generation into an unhappy squeeze, with the result that it will be eaten up by the stress. It's a highly visual image all right, but it leaves no room for love and suggests only that caring for loved ones is hard. "Care giver" is a neutral medical word, which describes one's activity adequately but is also devoid of emotional content. Until a better term comes along, I will use it with that reservation.

Even our grandchildren were already grown up when my wife and I started looking more intensively after Mutti. She had lived alone, entertained, been a regular Temple-goer, and traveled everywhere by public transportation. Then, after becoming a centenarian and shortly after her graduation, she fell and broke her thigh, was operated on, fell again, had another fracture, and all too quickly made the descent from total mobility to a walker, then to a wheelchair, and finally to confinement in a hospital bed. It sounds like an easy progression, but it was not. Her independence evaporated as her infirmity increased, until in the end she required constant attention, day and night. Her visitors began to diminish in number, and though our children helped and the other grandchildren came from afar from time to time, Elizabeth and I were the chief care givers. The ultimate responsibility was of course mine. In the final year of her life I visited her just about every day I was in town, looked after the four women who attended her, and met the usual exigencies that such situations inevitably entail—but it never became a burden. Only afterwards did I realize how much energy this demanded of me. Everything in life has its price, and even love and duty take their toll. I did not find it out for myself until Mutti was gone, a few days short of her 103rd birthday.

There are probably many millions of people whose experience resembles mine. To be sure, no two situations are alike, yet a common strand is observable. Social workers and gerontologists give us a hand by letting us understand the way the old face the inevitable and how they see their children's responsibility. I was unaware of any of this and approached my mother's decline with innocence and ignorance. Of course, I had much contact with experts like nurses, doctors, and social workers, but though I myself was eighty years old at the time, I knew little about geriatrics and had to learn a lot of basics, like how to put a wheelchair into my car. What I never learned, however, was the way my mother viewed all of this. She had never been a truly happy person, and her last years of restricted living did not improve on that tendency. It was clear that she expected me to be there when she needed me, and I expected the same of myself.

There is a tremendous difference between giving care to children and giving it to parents. For one thing, relatively few parents neglect their growing children, while a lot of children are neglectful of their aging parents—especially when the latter are believed to be adequately taken care of in residences for the aged or nursing homes. Another and obvious difference is the age of the care giver: It is easier when you are still young and harder when you are older. The third difference is often overlooked, and only in retrospect did I obtain the proper perspective. It has to do with being self-critical, and this deserves some explanation.

Once little toddlers lose their novelty and become children striving for independence, we begin to be critical of them (and they of us as well). We think we know their weaknesses and, often years later, ask ourselves why in this or that respect we as parents failed them. But such thoughts will likely be fleeting, and in most families parents continue to love their off-spring and vice versa. The scenario changes when we care for our parents. While we are busy doing it we don't give it much thought, but when they die we can and will assess the past. I did and reluctantly came to the con-clusion that though I had faithfully looked after my mother, I could have done better. Unfortunately, death leaves us without a means of correction. We may have a similar sense with our children, but there is room for doing better wih them later, while death closes that door forever. This irreversible closure always seems to leave a trace of guilt in the survivors, and we Jews believe that we have been fed an extra portion of it with our mothers' milk. I remember what happened when, fifty years ago, my Dad died while visit-ing my brother in Fargo, N.D. He had a heart attack during the night and died instantly. For years Mutti blamed herself for having given him beans for supper. Guilt has no feet, but it surely has a way of getting to you quick-ly.

I was intrigued to read a brief essay by an art historian about her role as care giver to her mother:

> I visited my mother almost every day. If I was tied up . . . my husband would see her. Every Friday night we picked her up for Shabbat dinner . . . The nurturing role that Mother played with her three children when we were young, was reversed when she grew older. She became ever more dependent on me, although she fought hard to maintain control over her affairs. . . .
>
> The routine of our life—daily visits, Friday dinners, constant chauffeuring—was rudely shattered . . . when Mother fell and broke her hip. . . . It became apparent that she could no longer function independently. . . . Perhaps my visits also helped assuage my guilt...

The author could have been writing my own experience. It was almost word for word the same. From which I deduce (not scientifically, the sample being so small) that this describes in essence what takes place in many a family. The parent reverts to being a child, helpless and dependent, and however much the children do, it will always leave room for a residue of guilt with them. It's not easy to be a parent, and it's not easy to be a child.

Maybe it is good that we have no precise knowledge of what lies ahead. Schiller phrased it succinctly in one of his poems, where (broadly rendered) he says: "Ignorance [of the future] is life, while knowledge [of it] is death.

Our lack of knowledge extends to another, somewhat related, area of living. Often I was called on to give advice in this typical situation: Someone has died, and the question is whether a certain old member of the family should be told. "It will kill him or her" is the fear that is often expressed with genuine concern. "He or she will never know."

With very few exceptions, my advice (following Jewish tradition) has been the opposite. Especially when the relationship is close, oldsters are entitled to know that their child, grandchild, or best friend has preceded them to the grave. I have yet to learn of a single case where imparting such knowledge has killed anyone. The fact is that older people's psychic structure is not as frail as others may think; on the contrary, emotions tend to flatten out as we age, and when it comes to death and misfortune, we have seen too much of it in our time to let it shock us fatally. Children are often amazed at their elders' apparent equanimity when receiving bad news. Long life has toughened them and has provided an emotional armor. We have no right to judge how others will deal with information they are entitled to have. But if they are not told and then find out, they will indeed be deeply wounded. (That applies also to knowing the nature of one's illness, but that concerns everyone, not just the old.)

Philip Roth writes about his own father's reaction to the fact that, when the son had undergone a serious operation, the old man had not been told but learned about it later. The father remembered this bitterly on his deathbed. "'I should have been there,' he repeated angrily, even with fury."

Left Behind

Right now I pay one price for becoming old: I am losing my friends. One was my doctor, one my lawyer; my classmates of the seminary are checking out, and in the bulletin of the congregation in St. Paul where I served for thirteen years, only the names in the obituary column are known to me. At a recent convention of the Central Conference of American Rabbis I was the oldest in attendance. Among the 400 or so who did attend, I knew fewer than 50—and that was the organization I had once headed as its president.

"Of course," someone will tell me, "you should have expected that. Get yourself friends who are young and it won't happen to you quite so often." True. My mother knew how to do it, but I don't. Maybe that's because I'm surrounded by books rather than people and kept busy with ideas rather than company. As I write this I know that my observation is skewed and that I am probably trying to cover up a fissure in my personality. Still, the fact remains that familiar faces are fewer and the young are absent from my everyday life—and alas, our grandchildren have never lived in Toronto. Thus, grandparenthood is rarely hands-on for us, and when we see some of our friends surrounded by their grandchildren we are strongly reminded that, except for our daughter, we are a long-distance family.

Whenever I think of our shrinking convoy, Elizabeth's mother comes to my mind. She had been living in Cincinnati and had been widowed for more than half a century. She had childhood friends who framed her life and kept the canvas of her years taut. But as she aged, her friends, one by one, left for the unknown, and when she came to visit us one spring, a film of sadness overlay her demeanor. As she was ready to say good-bye, she hesitated for a moment, as if to postpone what she wanted to convey. "You know," she finally ventured, "it isn't fun any more. They're all gone." We tried to cheer her up with thoughts of her children, grandchildren, and the first great-grandchild. "It isn't the same," she said. She left, and we never saw her again before the Angel of Death paid her a visit. She had not suffered from any traceable illness; she simply felt that she had enough of life.

For us who mourned her, she had left a lesson we could not forget. Becoming old has its promise and its price. The price is the loneliness of the survivor, and the greater the love, the greater the loneliness. Some will seek refuge in group living, hoping that it will lessen the pain. All of us who are temporary survivors are candidates for this trauma. Meanwhile we are challenged to make the most of the days still left to us and to live them to the fullest. Our memories represent the capital of the years we have lived; but we must not allow the past to burden us with an unbearable mortgage of yesterdays. I once had a congregant who after losing her spouse visited the cemetery every day of the year. Sorrow became the center of her existence, with the present becoming a wasteland. One day I gave her a poem that I thought might speak to her pain:

> If I should die and leave you here a while,
> Be not like others, sore undone, who keep
> Long vigil by the silent dust and weep.
> For my sake turn again to life and smile,
> Nerving thy heart and trembling hand to do
> That which will comfort other souls than thine;
> Complete these dear unfinished tasks of mine,
> And I, perchance, may therein comfort you.

The few lines had a miraculous impact on her. She cherished them and soon knew them by heart. "Now" assumed a new urgency for her, as it must for all of us who are left behind, bidding us to harvest the fruits of time.

What is it to grow old?
Is it to lose the glory of the form,
The luster of the eye?
Is it for Beauty to forgo her wreath?
Yes; but not this alone.
Matthew Arnold

I am old-fashioned enough not to enter
the meat market of self-revelation
that voyeurs love to read about.

Letting Go While Hanging In

A New Reality

While working on this book I would quite often be asked about the subject I was writing about. "Being old," I would say, which more often than not would engender a response like this: "Old? Not you! What do you know about it?"

To hear this is nice, flattering and reassuring. They want to tell me that I'm still with it and haven't yet entered the state of physical and/or mental decrepitude which they deem to be the signs of being "old." They fall into the common trap of looking at oldness as a state of debility, rather than a period of often very slow decline. I'd like to think that so far I have been traveling in the slow lane but have already covered enough distance to garner first-hand experience in the land of the aged.

People who have suffered from arthritis or strokes, broken a hip, had a heart attack or an operation for arterial blockage, had to stop playing the piano or tennis or golf, or had a serious setback of one kind or another have no trouble affirming that they are not what they used to be. But though so far I have been fortunate enough not to have suffered lasting and debilitating restrictions of my life style, I too am not my former self. If I were, medical journals would rush to write me up. Maybe if I did weight lifting and frequented the fitness center I would slow the downward trend, but since I get bored with even the simple exercises I am supposed to do in order to feel stronger, nature has its own way with me. My apparent unwillingness to slow the process down is part of the decline.

So my fingers have made arthritis an unwanted but permanent guest; my muscles are shrinking, though I am far from Shakespeare's devastating description of the "shrunk shank" or the "tattered coat upon a stick" of W. B. Yeats. My serve is weakening and aces have become a memory; my tee shots refuse to pass the 200-yard marker and increasingly explore unknown territory; and my rotator cuffs invite physiotherapy and cortisone injections. I put up a good front and am just happy to pursue my athletic hobbies, albeit with increasing injury-related interruptions. When, after the game, someone in the locker room asks me, "How did you play?" mine is a stock reply: "I *played*!" I am glad when I am asked so that I can give that answer, for it reminds me that, above all, I should be grateful. And I am.

I was a practicing clergyman long enough to know a goodly number of hospitals and care facilities (nursing homes, seniors' residences, homes for the aged, etc.) that reached a level of excellence because they never cease to care for their patients as individuals. But I also visited enough institutions where "inmates" were warehoused, reduced to inactivity and depression, not to be aware of my own good fortune until now. Still, the worm of time has not passed me by; it nibbles away, bit by bit, at my strength and—perhaps most important—at my desires.

It took me quite a while to become aware of it. Some desires that were important yesterday have become less so, or even unimportant. Possessions fall into that category. In a recent book, in a chapter also called "Letting Go," I related how we disposed of many things, including significant parts of our library, when we sold our home that we had inhabited for three and a half decades. I recalled that giving away my cherished acquisitions of yesteryear caused not an ounce of regret, let alone pain. After all, even books are only things that join the grand parade of desire/acquisition/possession/discard. They had their day of bringing me enjoyment, and now they trekked elsewhere and found a new abode.

Since then I have learned that such painless letting go of things has another dimension. Having grown old we have, instead of acquiring things, acquired a growing indifference to them because our desire to have them has progressively diminished, to the point of disappearance. Aging means acquiring a different set of priorities. For instance, though we have more time at our disposal than ever before, we go out less and less frequently; the comfort of staying home rings bells we didn't hear before. Part of this change is no doubt due to our lessened energy level, but also, we don't feel that we have to be seen on occasions we would not have missed in earlier days. We no longer need to prove ourselves or impress anyone, not even ourselves. We relax more successfully now than we ever did, for the yoke of society's Great Chase and the time constraints that go with it have been lifted from our necks, especially mine. The obligations we assume these days are voluntary; we may choose not to take them on.

I wonder sometimes why the young (particularly when driving their cars) are so impatient—after all, they have the greater portion of their lives still before them, and gaining a few seconds does not count for much. It is different with us: Our time is limited, yet we older people are the ones that are likely to be patient. Then again, bending time to one's will may be a thrill to the youthful driver, but hardly for us.

Not only time but money, too, seems have have changed its value for us. While formerly we would pay close attention to a dollar spent, we now increasingly tend to indulge ourselves—though there are limits. The memory of the Great Depression seems imbedded in our subconscious and keeps us from over-indulgence. We were never big on fancying nice clothes, a large home, or a fashionable car, and have never envied those who liked and owned them. Even so, we did not then, nor do we now, denigrate ordinary pleasures that are occasionally expressed in beautiful things.

Circling the Wagons

This expression arose in America's pioneer days, when migrants to the West arranged their wagons in a circle as a defensive measure against enemy attacks. I sometimes think of us oldsters in this fashion, though we fear no external dangers, and in any case, it takes more than oldness to enable one couple to circle anything. Still, the metaphor has application for us, as it has for others at this stage of life, when we try to guard against unknown inimical forces.

In fact, we live in a state of growing isolation. We hardly entertain at all, and when we do we take our guests to a restaurant or the golf club. Besides, Elizabeth declared one day that she had cooked long enough, and our children helped to make her decision feasible. Carol, our son Jonathan's wife, stocks our refrigerator at regular intervals, so we are supplied with cooked meals for some six weeks, and all we have to do is to call on the microwave oven for assistance in getting them to the table. Our daughter, Judith, has become our hostess for the traditional Shabbat dinner on Friday nights—an idea that some of our friends reject for themselves. "I'm never letting go of Friday nights and Passover seder," they say with firm conviction. Elizabeth, on the other hand, believes that handing over these traditional occasions is good for both generations.

Letting go has other aspects. Though we live in a city rich with cultural opportunities we have drifted into taking less and less advantage of them. The world-renowned Shakespeare and Shaw festivals are beckoning from Stratford and Niagara-on-the-Lake, but somehow these lovely places seem to have moved farther away, in the same way as steps are said to have become steeper than they used to be and floors lower when you try to bend down (this is what I hear has happened and is no doubt something I will soon discover for myself). We finally resubscribed to a music season with the Toronto Symphony, went out for dinner before the concerts—all very nice, yet somehow the offerings failed to connect with us. We did not renew our subscriptions.

Public television, with its staid and mostly sensible programs, has become our visual habitat, and its occasional wonderfully crazy shows add to our enjoyment. It takes so little energy to turn the knob or click the monitor, and we used to wonder why so many people find this a welcome means of spending empty time. Not for us, we said with a voice tinged by superiority, not until now anyway. We love seeing *Hamlet, Cyrano,* or *Guys and Dolls* come our way on the tube, along with ballet and modern dance, all of which finds the two of us watching with peace of mind and ease of body. They have not yet invented theater seats to match the chairs we have at home. That of course is the attraction of renting video tapes, but this is a habit that we have not yet made our own, though we have talked about adopting this pleasant means of entertaining ourselves when this book is finished and my wife's latest work has been published.

Both of us, in our separate studies, listen to good music, even as we do when motoring. In Toronto, three FM stations bring us splendid offerings all day long. In addition, I am and will always be an inveterate sports fan. When Wimbledon or the British Open rolls around I'm there (in front of some TV set, that is) to watch my favorite players. Also, I have to confess, there's the History channel, quite often featuring war movies. When they are good I am glued to the screen, for they recall a phase in my life that shaped me more than I had realized at the time. When they show a combat soldier returning home, tears fill my eyes, something that does not embarrass me one bit. I went to see Steven Spielberg's *Saving Private Ryan*. Though I was still in the States on D-Day 1944, I saw enough trench warfare later on so that I watched the cinematic recreation of the slaughter on Omaha Beach as something to which I could relate. Yesterday is still with me, though it is now more than fifty years ago, and I remind myself how much more the past must continue to be present with a survivor of the Holocaust.

And where does reading come in? "I'm saving it up for when I'm retired" expresses the thought of sporadic readers. They usually find that being old does not bring with it a thirst for reading. In fact, most of us oldsters are just what and who we always were. We change to some degree, slowing down mostly, but essentially we remain the same. If you were a reader before, you'll probably do more reading now; exceptions will be rare. Besides, reading takes concentration, and concentration requires an expenditure of energy of which we have less and less as we go along.

When we moved from our house I made sure to take along certain books that I had promised myself I would finally get to read. No such luck; I have not had the time. That is of course the most often-heard excuse for not reading, not volunteering, not looking after one's offspring or one's parent, and the like. "Having time" is not primarily measured by the chronometer. Instead it represents a shortcut statement of priorities. Assuming that the potential reader has no trouble with her or his eyesight, and therefore reading books is one of the choices she or he has, "I haven't got the time" means "I've got no time for reading, I have more important things to do." There will be time for golf, pinochle, TV, or whatever the priorities of leisure may be. The long and the short of it is that the simple and truthful answer to the question "What do you read?" would be, "I'm not a reader." But that does not sound acceptable. One has to be careful, there may be an aspiring intellectual in hearing distance.

Having made the case for reading—and I mean books, not newspapers, magazines, trade journals, or Internet information—I have to admit that my wife and I rarely read primarily for pleasure, as once we did. Of course we do read, but usually not for relaxation or inspiration; we are writers and we do have reading priorities. They include study in our fields of research: my wife in genealogy and I in the area of my current work. This means, in fact, reading a lot, but within the narrow confines of the subject matter on hand. It happens that in writing this book I read quite widely (and I hope the result reflects it), and much of what I garnered was highly stimulating. I would never have taken to hand such books as André Gide's *Journals* or Bessie Ellen Richardson's *Old Age Among the Ancient Greeks*, to give just two examples out of the many you will find mentioned in my Notes.

I usually take a book or two along with me when I travel, provided the print is large enough, a feature that purveyors of paperbacks, and especially mystery stories, rarely provide. I have struck my own balance, and I know I'm fortunate to have any choices at all. For me, old age has brought restrictions but also a frame of mind more attuned to opportunities I formerly overlooked.

Yesterday we took health for granted; we do not any more. As noted above, we've had warnings and incidents, as if to let us know that time intends to exacts its toll. We eventually adjust to restrictions, unaccustomed fatigue, and a lowering of the energy level. None of this has been sudden, but when I sit still and think about my life, I know it has changed in a number of ways and not least of all has brought me a kind of serenity I did not always possess. When I step on the balcony, overlooking the luscious ravine below, I listen to the leaves rustling in the tree tops . They must have rustled in this way since day one, but I never heard them before. This auditory discovery may also be understood as a metaphor: I perceive some things more clearly than I ever did before—the vagaries of old age among them—

and I am beginning to understand what a famous 63-year-old wrote a little over two thousand years ago.

Cicero Revisited

Marcus Tullius Cicero, in his day one of the most influential men in Rome, would not yet have qualified for Social Security, if it had been in existence in his time. But by the standards of his age (the first century BCE) he belonged to the aged, life expectancy then being about thirty years. I am beginning to comprehend what he had to say, though I am more than two decades older than he was when he wrote the Occident's first book on aging. He did not quarrel with life's downward spiral, on the contrary, he presented four separate reasons why old age was a time to let go yet held much to be grateful for. Though his words have a muffled ring to them and his arguments are quite self-serving, one should remember that in writing on this subject he was a pioneer and stood on no one's literary shoulders.

I find there are four reasons for old age being thought unhappy. First, that it withdraws us from active employments; second, that it enfeebles the body; third, that it deprives us of nearly all physical pleasures; fourth, that it is the next step to death.

On #1, withdrawal from employments. In modern terms, this would mean being excluded by society from working at a job and being condemned in the bargain as obsolete, superfluous, and costly (the worst crime of all). Said the Roman sage:

The great affairs of life are not performed by physical strength, or activity, or nimbleness of body, but by deliberation, character, expression of opinion.

Translated into today's concepts: Our inner qualities are what counts. Each one of us sets his or her own standards. Do not let others (including society) contort your scale of values. We do not have to be satisfied with the rejection we often meet and meekly accept it as a fact of life. True, our spirit is our primary measuring tape, especially as we age, but we are also part and parcel of the society in which we live. We have organizations of older people that mostly try to protect our financial stake, but as a group we have so far have not mustered the energy to gain for ourselves the kind of recognition and respect accorded to other minorities. We still have our voices, and speaking together we have a chance of being heard.

On #2, enfeeblement of body. Here is the gist of Cicero's comments:

> Bodily strength is wanting to old age, but neither is bodily strength demanded from the old. Use what you have, and whatever you may chance to be doing, do it with all your might.

Translation update: Do not measure yourself by younger folk. As little as twenty-five years from now, Tiger Woods will not hit the ball as far as he does now, however much he visits the fitness center to maintain his prowess. Flowers bloom for a relatively short time, and so does our physical vigor. Yet it is well to remember that in certain respects the older young, say those in their thirties and even forties, show greater endurance in mountain climbing, marathon races, and other prolonged efforts than their juniors, who excel in explosive bursts of energy like hitting a golf ball or clearing the hurdles in a 400-meter race. I have read of 80-year old marathon runners and long-distance cyclists of the same age, but none of their contemporaries is likely to press 200 kilograms. We can still do a lot, and for the important demands of ordinary living most of us do all right. My heart goes out to those who are suffering from debilitating conditions, and it is our duty to see to it that they obtain effective care in a dignified environment. They are the relatively few unfortunate ones whom aging has dealt a bad hand, and we owe it to ourselves to assist them in any way we can. Contrary to public impression, the great majority of the old live at home, alone or with families, or spend much or all of their time in pleasant climes. Most of them would say with Tennyson:

> Tho' much is taken, much abides; and tho'
> We are not now that strength which in old days
> Moved earth and heaven; that which we are we are,
> One equal temper of heroic hearts,
> Made weak by time and fate, but strong in will
>   To strive, to seek, to find, and not to yield.

Cicero deals with the same subject with sweeping judgment when he says: "Fools impute their own frailties to old age." Will, desire, and persistence do help when we are struck with debility, but they have a limit, and those who complain about them are not necessarily fools.

On #3, losing our physical pleasures. A tricky subject that Cicero treated without becoming too autobiographical. That suits me fine, for I am old-fashioned enough not to enter the meat market of self-revelation that voyeurs love to read about. I do not know whether the famous orator was all dried up, as they say, for he does not tell us and only asserts that sensual pleasure is overrated anyway:

> Intellect is the best gift of nature or God: to this Divine gift there is nothing so inimical as pleasure. For when appetite is our master, there is no place for self-control; nor when pleasure reigns supreme can virtue hold its ground. . . . For pleasure blinds the eyes of the mind.

Here the rhetorician shows his hand. His argument might succeed in a spirited lecture; it does not when set down on paper. For he posits pleasure and intellect as opposites that cannot live with each other; in his view it is likely that either one or the other rules us. That is, of course, true only when someone is purely sensual and feels pleasure to be the crown and purpose of living. That is why teenagers, in addition to their intellectual immaturity, are not fit philosophers; sex doth blind their minds more often than not. But philosophers have been known to be in love and (though they rarely tell us) probably have enjoyed pleasurable sex.

Given the longevity expectations of his time, Cicero at 63 was biologically my age. He spoke primarily to men and of men; women were not his primary audience. And when it comes to sex, we need to remember that men can usually procreate as long as they are capable of having intercourse; while women after menopause cannot. But while men's sexual potency decreases with the years and will eventually disappear altogether, women's ability to enjoy sex does not. Life does have its balance, even here.

On #4, the nearness of death. Cicero writes:

> What a poor dotard must be he who has not learnt in so long a life that death is not a thing to be feared! Death is either to be totally disregarded if it entirely extinguishes the soul, or is even to be desired if it bring him to where he is to exist forever. A third alternative cannot possibly be discovered. The author then goes on to affirm the immortality of the soul.

Unfortunately, after finishing his treatise on being old, Cicero was not destined to enjoy many more days. He had bitterly attacked the members of the governing triumvirate, because instead of restoring Rome to its freedoms they pursued the very aims that had cost Julius Caesar his life. Cicero had welcomed the dictator's death, and in a letter to a friend he suggested that the same fate be meted out to Octavian (Caesar's adopted son), because he too threatened to wield total power. Somehow Octavian learned of Cicero's missive and saw to it that the injudicious writer was hunted down and killed. His head and hands were exhibited in the very forum where he had scored his greatest oratorical victories, while Octavian went on, as Cicero had feared, to become Rome's supreme ruler and called himself Augustus. (Moral: If you want to live into old age watch what you write, or at least be sure to use encrypted e-mail.)

The Ciceronian defense of old age is easy to read. But, for my taste, it is a bit too defensive and too rhetorical. I know enough of the great master's art of rhetoric to be aware that argument from the platform (secular or religious) frequently falls on its face if it becomes an academic lecture. The latter exposes all sides of the issue at hand, the former strongly stresses the points the speaker wants to get across. Cicero defends the positive aspects of aging but says nothing about its burden. Maybe the public was getting tired of the old men in the Senate and therefore made it possible for 32-year-old Octavian to grasp the reins and crown himself Rome's first emperor. He managed to outlast his enemies as well as the life expectancy of his time by surviving to the ripe old age of 77.

Doing and Being

As I have tried to show earlier, identity is a problem for many of us oldsters. We cannot quickly answer the question "What do you do?" or the often unspoken but implied "What do you do with yourself these days?" We are measured, classified, and accepted or rejected by what we are doing or not doing. Formerly this was primarily a male problem; now—with an ever larger number of women old enough to have retired from the work force—it affects the majority of the aged.

Since "doing" is identified with paid labor, the fact is that most of us oldsters are not "doing" anything, which has left a lot of us drifting rudderless in the social sea. I am not totally exempt from this perception, even though I do work in the accepted meaning of the word. For writing (like painting) is considered by most people primarily a hobby, except maybe for journalists and writers of advertising copy. I can just imagine someone answering the "what are you doing" question by saying "I'm a poet," to which the response will likely be either a superior smile or "Oh, really?!" which means, "So you aren't really doing anything."

In fact, filling one's day is a problem for many; boredom is a cruel enemy. For a long time I have wondered why so relatively few retired people volunteer their services to some sector of the community. A multitude of organizations could benefit from our participation. The Hebrew language has a special expression for such activity: Doing a mitzvah. It bears the stamp of the Divine: visiting the sick. comforting the bereaved, feeding the hungry, providing shelter for the homeless—the catalogue is endless. The reward for such response to the needs of others is the very doing itself, which is the way our tradition phrases its encouragement. Two examples come to mind:

Like many other cities, Toronto has a Distress Centre, where people who are in deep trouble and contemplating suicide can reach a willing ear. I am familiar with the organization, having served as a director for some time. I have unlimited admiration for some of the volunteers who are on call during night hours, when despair seems more likely to descend on potential victims. It requires devotion, training, a fair amount of psychic energy, and the sacrifice of a night's sleep. But, I have been told on more than one occasion, the opportunity of possibly saving someone's life is a challenge second to none and richly rewards the one who responds to it.

I will also never forget the time when my wife underwent a worrisome operation. Our children were with me in the special room set aside by the hospital for those who wait for the end of the surgery and the subsequent report of the doctor. A volunteer, perhaps a few years older than I, was with us, attending to whatever needs we might have. His great contribution to our mental welfare was his being there for us. He had experience with anxious families, of whom we certainly were one. I had a chance to explore his own feelings about his volunteer work and found him a truly fulfilled human being. Eventually, when the surgeon came and brought us good news, the gentle volunteer was able to rejoice with us. I forget what his former paid occupation had been; I know that what he did now was invaluable and the doing of it his rich reward. More than that, he reinforced a great lesson: Being there is sometimes the core of doing.

Which recalls something that happened to me over fifty years ago, when we lived in the Chicago area. In the middle of the night our telephone rang. A friend of ours was calling, but I could hardly understand the muffled words that came over the wire. Finally I grasped the horrible news: her five-year-old daughter had died in her sleep. No illness, no warning—the Angel of Death had entered unannounced. We hurried to our friends' home and sat with them until dawn. We said nothing; we just were there. Years later the mother confided this to us: "I'll never forget what you did for us that night. Just sitting there with us, in our indescribable state of shock, was invaluable. You became friends for life. But if you would have tried to comfort us I might have thrown you out."

The older I become the better I understand the deeper meaning of *being there*. Martin Buber, in his *Dialogue,* tells of two men who are strangers to each other. They sit together in silence, yet inexplicably communicate with each other. Elsewhere Buber related an experience he himself had had. A philosopher-colleague had spent a day as his house guest. The night before he left, the two men sat in silence before the fireplace. The hours passed, no words were spoken. When the morning light broke the spell, the guest took his departure, saying something to this effect: "Thank you for the wonderful conversation we had last night." Being there can be a form of conversation.

When we age we have a chance to be ourselves, which is "being there" when it is needed most. In earlier days we are caught in the treadmill of trying to accomplish something; now that we are on the sidelines of the workaday world, we can fill many a waking hour with just being there for our families, our friends, and, through the intermediary of some religious institution or social organization, for strangers. Our identity becomes real as we meet someone else in a meaningful way. Buber put it succinctly: A person becomes "I" only through "Thou." South Africa's Kaffir express this insight to perfection in everyday life. When they greet each other they say, "I see you."

I am not without experience in volunteering. It is often not exciting, and then suddenly it is, and all the hours spent seem more than worth it. I give of myself somewhat less these days, but if ever I could no longer fill my day with writing, reading, and a bit of exercise, the volunteer sector of the community would see me once again more frequently. As long as one has the capacity to do something for others, boredom can never become a fearsome visitor.

"To be" means also to be aware of oneself in the fullest sense: I am alive and, feeling good about it, do not hesitate to give it expression. I noted earlier that, when I am asked how I did in a tennis or golf game, I answer, "I played! " Similarly, when someone greets me with "How are you?"—not really much more than "Hello!"—I may respond with "I *am*!" and mean just that. I am grateful to be here, and no morning or evening prayer I say omits that awareness.

Everyone is aware of the price of growing old, since one observes it frequently as it exacts its toll in others. But the privilege of aging is something we have to experience for ourselves. It is not visible to the eye, for it is a new state of our spirit: Changed priorities, reordered values, serenity and, hopefully, a pervasive sense of gratitude.

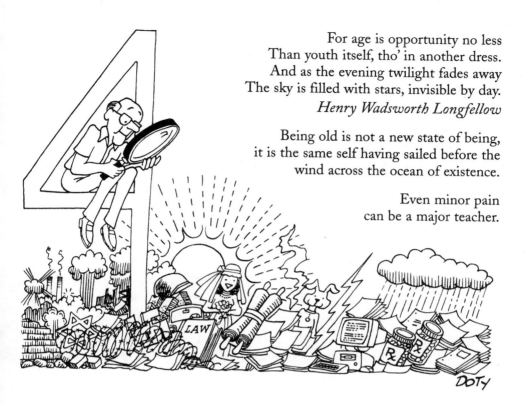

For age is opportunity no less
Than youth itself, tho' in another dress.
And as the evening twilight fades away
The sky is filled with stars, invisible by day.
Henry Wadsworth Longfellow

Being old is not a new state of being,
it is the same self having sailed before the
wind across the ocean of existence.

Even minor pain
can be a major teacher.

The View From the Tower

Using Spyglasses, Retrospector & Analyzer on Myself

Being old is life's final halting place. It has one advantage over those crucial moments in youth and middle age, when we make decisions about the direction we want to take. We choose our major study subject, the job(s) we take, the spouse(s) we acquire, the child(ren) we decide to bring into the world, and the geographic locale(s) where our future will be played out. All of these and other personal watersheds turn up in the midst of growth, change and time constraints; we cannot stand still long enough, nor do we have the perspective to consider all options. We are always on the run, sometimes slowed to a trot and then again pursuing life and its evasive goals in full flight. Like marathon runners, we see who is ahead of us and occasionally look back over our shoulder to gauge the pace of the pursuers. Meanwhile our legs move, the heart keeps on pumping, and the mind concentrates on keeping us going. But somewhere, past the middle of the contest, a lot of runners take a brief break. They wonder whether the effort is really worth it and whether they should continue. Maybe they should change course, seeing they did not do as well as they had hoped, finding themselves disappointed with their performance and suddenly wondering whether their competitive goals need redefining. So some drop out, others get back, and doubt slows the pace of others. To their surprise they find that many of their competitors took the same kind of respite, with similar results. It occurs to them that the race is not that important after all, as long as they manage to reach the goal line, which is usually marked with a big 65.

That's more or less the time when "young old age" begins. From now on it is a walk, not a run, and having paid our dues and received the order of merit called "old," we can do what we never had a chance to do: We can take a view of our own life from the Tower of Time that we can find in our own neighborhood. It usually has lots of stories. An elevator gets us to the observation platform, where we find an astonishing array of equipment: spyglasses that examine our past objectively; retrospectors that tell us what was good, bad, or indifferent; analyzers that examine our present and future status. All equipment has a warning attached that its use is at our own peril and that the results are not guaranteed by the manufacturer and, besides, have a margin of error amounting to 50 percent. Still, this platform and the ability to use the machinery represent a privilege that the old have over their younger contemporaries, who rarely take the time to visit this extraordinary place.

Not surprisingly, admission to the Tower, which is usually, but not always, reserved for the old, is not free. I purchased my ticket, reached the observation area, and started using the spyglasses, retrospectors, and analyzers that the management had readied for me. I was warned of the unreliability of the observations, signed a waiver that protected the Tower against any lawsuit, swallowed some pills to calm my nerves, and began looking.

First image: "Patience! What and whom you see may not seem to picture scenes and people that you recognize. Stick with it; your eyes will clear and your comprehension improve. Good luck!"

Then I saw a young man who looked vaguely familiar. He was in his teens, of medium size, blond, and without distinguishing characteristics. I pressed the retrospector button in order to read his history.

Locale: Berlin, 1930. Middle-class family with two sons. The older one was ready to go university but had no idea which discipline to pursue. I heard his father suggest that with a law degree there would be many options later on. The young man said "Yes, sir!" and went to law school. He studied little, played chess and soccer instead, then took a quick course to prepare him for the exams.

The forward button stopped at Berlin, Fall 1933, six months into the Nazi regime. The young man had finished law school and passed his exams, but Hitler disqualified him because he was a non-Aryan. Entered the father, who suggested that the liberal Jewish seminary would be a good place to audit some courses, and meanwhile the German people would come to their senses and throw the rascals out. After that the young man could once again take up his law career. "Yes, sir!" he said. I noticed that he followed his father's advice quite readily, but it was unclear what he himself wanted from life.

Forward to Berlin, 1935. Hitler was getting stronger, not weaker, and the German people appeared cowed and compliant. The young man received an invitation from America to continue his studies at a rabbinical seminary and, at his father's suggestion accepted for two years only. Clearly, becoming a rabbi did not enter his mind, and the first thing he did in the States was to inquire at a law school—but he learned that he would have to start from scratch, which he found unappealing. Thereupon he dutifully took his course at the seminary in Cincinnati, where he waited for Hitler to return to painting houses. (The analyzer could not speculate on his future success. It did not have enough data on him, for he had not shown enough personal initiative so far and had drifted along, letting his father, the Nazis, and his new American environment make the decisions for him.) For some reason he was quite cocky and seemed interested mostly in girls and in playing tennis, which he did well.

Back to the retrospector. Berlin, 1937: Hitler had become Germany's dictator and the future for Jews, especially the young, became darker all the time. At his father's urging, the young man came home to take his brother with him back to America. The thought that a seventeen year old boy might have been able to make the journey by himself apparently did not occur to his parents, even as disobeying them had not occurred to the young man. (The analyzer called the trip back into the jaws of the Nazi sharks an "idiot's journey.") He was lucky. Nothing happened to him, and with his brother he left the country of their birth.

I had seen enough, for I was becoming upset. I had known for a while already that the young man was indeed my own younger self, but what I saw (and had confirmed by the analyzer) was not the way I had remembered my earlier years. It looked as if I had let myself be borne along by my father's direction and the shifting winds of circumstance.. Where were my free will, determination, and purpose? Was this the way the rest of my life had been traversed? Did I not decide of my own volition that I would pursue the vocation of a rabbi?

Christian ministers often say of their reason for becoming clerics that "the Lord called them." I remember no such illumination. Instead, I must have grown spiritually through my studies without being aware of it. Somehow it began to dawn on me that I might be ordained, especially since my visit to Germany had finally made it clear that there would be no return to political sanity. Until then I had drifted along—suspended between the (unfortunately wrong) expectations of my parents and the pleasant environment of Hebrew Union College.

At that time also, I fell in love with a young lady I had met by chance and was married six months later. No drifting there; it was the first real choice I had made for myself, to hitch my wagon to the new star I had discovered. Were love and marriage the final push that moved me from drifting along in my studies to saying yes to entering the ministry? I do not know; I only know that my parents had not planned it that way, and neither had I. In subsequent years, until I reached old age, I did make some important life decisions (like moving to new positions and cities, or taking on national and international responsibilities), but in between I did much drifting. The analyzer would probably inform me that during these periods I had lived once again for long stretches on automatic pilot. Had I changed now, with the passing years?

That question is the reason I have constructed this whole metaphor. For as we grow into old age we have probably made some vital decisions, but after each of them become increasingly limited in our choices: what to do or not to do; to move or to stay; to live independently or in a group facility. There is no reason to mourn these constrictions, for probably most of us have made few important life choices. These were always limited to some degree or other, and in between we drifted with the current for years or decades at a time. Therefore the limitations we now perceive are best met with graceful acceptance rather than with sorrow and regret. We have all drifted before, and now we have drifted into oldness. Younger folk will rarely perceive this truth, but we oldsters have a chance to see ourselves from the Tower of Time. This is the bonus we enjoy, and with it comes the opportunity to draw certain conclusions for ourselves, and primarily for our own state of mind.

The fact is, we are still the same people. Being old is not a new state of being, it is the same self having sailed before the wind across the ocean of existence. In that sense, as one author put it, each one of us remains an "ageless self."

> [The aged] do not relate to aging or chronological age as a category of experience or meaning. To the contrary, when old people talk about themselves, they express a sense of self that is ageless— an identity that maintains continuity despite the physical and social changes that come with old age. Old people know who they are and what matters to them now, and, as they think about these subjects, they may, in passing, describe themselves as "feeling old" in one context and "feeling young" in another.

Green Bananas

Everyone knows that our will influences the way our body functions. The surgeon who has operated on you may tell you that recovery time is about ten days in the hospital and three weeks at home. Of course, the doctor cannot be sure; some heal more quickly than others. Any recuperative period mentioned to us is an estimate based on averages. But an individual person has usually a chance to improve the averages. People who go into the operation determined to withstand its rigors successfully and overcome its after-effects quickly are more likely to succeed on both counts than those beset by anxiety. In the struggle for physical wholeness, mind and will have their say.

Of course there is a limit; at some point your body tells you that have to go with what you have and that what you want is no longer possible. Every year I have to do with a little less, feel a little more fatigued and less ambitious, and injuries hang around as if they like me. Being aware of this decline has—strange as it may sound—helped me to appreciate each day. I accept that this is the way it is and meanwhile am grateful for what I have. I still possess a reservoir of zest, but I do not expend it helter-skelter. It is nonreplaceable capital.

Eighteen years ago, when I started writing short stories, it never occurred to me to question why I was so comfortable with this newly discovered medium. Now, having looked at myself from the Tower, I think I know. I first thought of writing fiction not long after quitting my job, when Elizabeth and I took a vacation in Spain. It was the first time in a long while that we had treated ourselves to such a luxury; most of our other travel had been work-related, though very enjoyable as well. But this time, just sitting still, talking, reading and thinking, I may have confronted my subconscious self with the fact that I had entered the last stage of my life. For seventeen years I had worked on the Torah commentary, my *magnum opus*, and clearly, any project of comparable length was out of the question from here on. I did not plan to write short stories; I had never ventured to write even a single one, but it happened in Spain. I wrote about a social scientist from Toronto who had an assignment and chose to work at it in the Iberian peninsula. Strange things happened to him and his labors, and the ending of the tale was quite unforeseen when I started writing. I certainly did not have myself consciously in mind when I wrote, but when I looked at it from the Tower it seemed clear that I myself was the story's chief character. It showed the scientist writing pretentious drivel that a shadowy visitor urged him to discard, which indeed he eventually did. Even now I am shocked at the possibility that it was I whom I was writing about. Still, this did not deter me from writing more stories, and later on I did write two full length novels.

There happened to be another aspect to writing that tale and the others that followed. They were all short-short stories. Was I evading longer-term commitments? Was I no longer buying green bananas because

I might not be around by the time they ripened? Was I afraid that I could not finish what I was starting to do? Perhaps I have stayed too long in the Tower and had forgotten that the equipment was only 50 percent reliable. Anyway, I plan on returning to writing more short stories when this book is finished, unless something unanticipated turns me to some other project. A few unpublished tales rest somewhere among my papers, and one publisher has already indicated an interest. The bananas I will buy from here on will be neither green nor overripe.

If and when I will write fiction again I'll do it on a computer, probably the very one I am presently using, an old laptop (black-and-white only—horrors!). For me, longhand is long gone, and the very thought of going back to it would cramp my fingers before I'd finish the first page. But I also know that my Macintosh is not happy with me. I type with two fingers only and have to look at the keyboard while doing it. I think my PowerBook 170 would love me more if I knew how to type the way schoolchildren can. So why do I not learn it now? After all, our dog of whom I wrote earlier, learned new tricks while quite elderly (I cannot tell whether calling him old would offend his memory as it would an average human being). There are self-teaching courses in typing with which I could struggle at home, so why not plunge in and use ten fingers instead of two? Because—it is just unappealing. Why, I do not really know. Anyway, typing at high speed might tempt me to write more, which for a variety of reasons I deem inadvisable. Two fingers it will remain, and I have herewith revealed yet another of my weaknesses.

Incidentally, since my PowerBook is old, it also meets the same rejection that we elderly humans have to face. On a recent trip to a computer hospital I was handed a slip of paper from the manufacturer, with the blunt information that spare parts from "obsolete" models would no longer be available. So here is an obsolete instrument used by an obsolete person— two negatives that try to amount to something positive.

The Ups and Downs of It All

Old age means striking your sails and drifting along most of the way to the final berth; it is easier that way and, if we are lucky and have reasonably good health on our side most of the time, it can be a lot of fun. So far I have been fortunate: I continue writing three or four hours a day and find it rewarding. To be sure, sometimes when I read over what I perpetrated the day before I wonder why I had so little judgment, and I will correct the chapter or restart the article from scratch. When things do not go my way I am likely to take it without great fuss, which is very different from the determination to right things where possible that marked my younger days.

For some reason my two-volume autobiography (one written as I turned 70, and the other 15 years later) mentioned the downside of aging only tangentially. Maybe, subconsciously, I tried to ward off the evil spirits of getting old. For we do not often talk about the personal problems of that process, just as several generations ago we did not talk of cancer or dying. Eventually cancer made its way into public consciousness through highly touted reports of new treatments, while dying became a subject for polite company only when, in 1969, Swiss physician Elisabeth Kübler-Ross wrote *On Death and Dying* and made the subject acceptable. More recently, Mitch Albom's *Tuesdays with Morrie* has raised the subject to best-seller status.

Books galore describe how to make the most of getting and being old. But most fall short of being totally open about it, perhaps because those who write about it are generally younger and gather their insights from observing others, or perhaps because publishers reject manuscripts they judge will be unpopular.

One angry writer belongs to the exceptions. Born in 1918 she has published what she calls "a contrary, even dour view" of growing old, and calls those who portray it as a time of fulfillment a lucky minority.

> Look closely: it is for most a time of inevitable loss, painful because we have grown so accustomed to the confident strides and gains of youth and maturity that when our decline begins, physically, psychically, intellectually, emotionally, we hardly notice. Our reach, characteristic of our best and brightest years, exceeds our weakened grasp. [The first thing we lose is our ambition, she continues, and the most lamentable is the erosion of hope.] Still, despite my dire description, we elderly persist with our canes, in our long-term care and miserable nursing homes and "rehabilitation" centers, and in our seats confronting the idiocies of the tube. In the short run, so to speak, we are all characters in "Waiting for Godot."

Her view is realistic, maybe too realistic for most publishers to give it space. For aging, in the best of circumstances, is indeed a process of personal deterioration, aside from the considerable social rejection that I will discuss later. I am aware of the advantages that old age brings me, but at the same time I am a realist, and realism tells me to make the best of the fact that the road leads downhill, regardless of whether I shut my eyes to it or open them wide. I prefer the latter, and thereby I learn a great deal about myself, allowing me to see where I am going rather than stumbling from one pothole to another, which may be called a form of old-age drifting. Those who know me think that I still have it all together. Not quite, and for once I can say I know better. My future, like anyone else's, is contracting inescapably, but I want to extract from it the best I possibly can.

Meanwhile, however, what yesterday was a minor muscle pull now starts a drawn-out process of slow healing. Increasingly, the healing becomes less and less complete, and pain—endurable, but nagging nonetheless—becomes a constant companion. I've learned to deal with it, so far, anyway. Fortunately, in comparison to life's enjoyments it remains minor, and for that too I am grateful. My off-and-on aches have also taught me increased awareness for what others, much worse off than I, have to meet every day. In addition to all else, even minor pain can be a major teacher.

Fortunately, this sense of acceptance seems to be widespread among my age group. Short of a major illness, I rarely hear my contemporaries complain about their aches, something that was borne out in a series of interviews that were assembled into a book called *Life Beyond 85 Years*. It showed how most of the oldest old—whom the authors call "survivors"—perceived their health as good and expressed contentment. Apparently, they had reached a stage of life when the usual stressors and demands had a decreasing effect on them.

Time Gives and Takes

The Holocaust brought to public attention a condition that had long been known to students of psychology, the so-called survivor syndrome. When grieving for the members of their family who breathed their last in the gas chambers or were dispatched by other means, the survivors were often beset by a sense of unease or even guilt. "Why did I survive when they did not?" became a tormenting question that had no answer. Even though I am not a Holocaust survivor in the strict meaning of the term—having escaped Germany in good time, before I could be shipped to a concentration camp—I am a survivor of warfare, having served with an American infantry division during its thrust into the Reich. To this day I dream occasionally about others dying, a comrade to whom I had spoken a few seconds earlier before he disappeared into nothingness, the gathering of the dead after the battle, their frozen corpses loaded on the trucks like cordwood.

Lately, similar sentiments crop up when a good friend or a member of the family succumbs, often suddenly. I remain behind, a survivor for the time being. Nowadays each death of the old I used to know diminishes my personal environment. That in itself is of course not new, for even when longevity was lower, the death of contemporaries who were old in terms of their time elicited feelings of growing loneliness among those remaining behind. For me, as the years roll by, the survivor syndrome is enlarged by a feeling of growing isolation. But the capacity to love remains and, as always, needs to be nourished and utilized.

Thus, time gives and it takes. Not long before he died, André Gide arrived at this rule, recorded in his journal:

To take things not for what they claim to be, but what they are;
Play the game with the hand one has;
Insist upon oneself as one is.

Obviously, Gide had used his daily journals as his personal Tower of Time.

PART TWO

SOCIETY LOOKING AT ME

We oldsters are quite unwilling to be cast on the societal ash heap as unusable antiques and be talked about accordingly.

No One Calls Me "Old"

Only Antiques Are Old

Do a little experiment. Ask an acquaintance: "Who in your family is old?" There will likely be a pause before an answer comes, and the conversation may go something like this:

Answer: "Well, grandma's pretty old."

Question: "Is she only 'pretty old' or really old?"

Answer: "Well, 'pretty old' describes her better."

Question: "Is there someone else you know who is old? If so, tell me why you call him or her old?"

Ask the same series of questions of several others and try to analyze what you have heard. Chances are that you will find people hesitant to call anyone "old" without toning it down a little. And if you have the nerve to ask whether the term fits them, most likely they will tell you, "I'm not old."

The point of this game? To give you some sense of how the word "old" is used when describing people. Formerly it had one connotation—mostly positive; and today it has another—mostly negative. Being old was one thing yesterday; it is quite something else today and will probably mean something else again to my as yet unborn great-grandchildren.

We now make a distinction between chronological and biological age-fixed numbers versus individual assessment. Chronologically a person may be said to be 85 years old and thereby fit a preconceived standard of decline, yet that same person may be, biologically speaking, full of vim and verve. If someone says, "Joe is 75 but not old," the chronological and biological elements are clearly distinguished from each other. While this distinction is an accurate description of reality, it really has no impact on the way society treats us. We aging folk are categorized as a group by chronology alone and treated accordingly, regardless of whether as individuals we fit the general perception of the old, and despite the fact that the aged are more heterogeneous in most ways than any other age group.

Being imprecise, the term "old" easily takes on different meanings in different ages, climes, and cultures and changes with its subject matter, as do all such words. A distance called "far" in little Luxembourg might mislead a visiting North American, who lives in a vast country. "Old" partakes of such differences and conveys one thing in conservative Ireland and another in the experimental culture of California.

Further, since "old" is used primarily as an adjective or predicate adjective, its meaning is also shaped by the noun it describes. A suit may be considered old after 5 years, while a Meissen plate becomes old only at 100. The life expectancy of a creature or the durability of a thing will determine when to call it old. Here is a haphazard collection of examples:

A bristle-cone pine may reach the age of 5,000, while the average life span of a redwood is a measly 1,000 years and that of a red maple 110. Cats average 15 years, dogs somewhat less; a tornado whizzes by in 10 minutes, and the average car muffler needs replacement after three years. A facelift does better, though not too much, and a dollar bill in the States is withdrawn from circulation after a year and a half. Professional basketball players need new shoes after two weeks, and the painted line in the middle of a busy highway will have to be repainted in less than half a year.

Some would avoid a definition altogether by saying, "You're only as old as you feel." That sounds good, but it says only that one should disregard chronological age and let biological age tell the whole story. Unfortunately, society is not prepared to agree; it likes its categories and stereotypes, and chronology serves both and thereby victimizes us aged folk.

Since "old" is such an imprecise word, can it be applied to people at all, seeing that we age so differently? Most dictionaries (which record public parlance) list numerous prejudicial meanings for the word when applied to people, for instance: "Exhibiting the physical or mental characteristics of age, antiquated, antediluvian, archaic, obsolete."

My own chronological definition would be: "'*Old*,' when applied to persons, describes those who have already lived most of their lives and have a fairly limited time span left to them."

By that definition, I am old, having passed my 86th birthday, even though in quite a few respects I can compete with, and occasionally even outdo, persons who are chronologically much younger than I. Still, the years ahead of me are relatively few and becoming fewer, and the end is something I think more and more about. It also makes it possible for me to take a good look not only at how I personally feel about this, but also at how others feel about me as an old person (though they will likely use other terms to describe me). Earlier this year, CARP (the Canadian Association of Retired Persons) published a list of the six most prevalent fables about the old:

> 1. *Age 65 marks the onset of old age.*
> [Legally, yes; but generally not otherwise.]
>
> 2. *The elderly are usually frail, senile or sick.*
> [As one doctor once said to my wife when, after a bad fall, she could not raise her arm: "What do you expect at your age?"]

3. Everyone becomes senile sooner or later.
[There is no such disease as senility; of those living past 80, fewer than 25 percent develop degenerative forms of brain damage.]

4. Older people are unproductive employees.
[Not so; they are in fact usually more adaptable and their absentee rate is often lower than that of younger workers.) In the U.S., discharging someone because of age is illegal.]

5. Older people just aren't sexy.
[Sophia Loren at 64 and Sean Connery at 69 are usually named in lists of the ten sexiest people.]

6. All old people think, act, and look the same.
[In fact, they represent the most diverse group of the population.]

Other fables could be added, for society's view of the aged is shot through with prejudice. Though for some time I had been well aware of it, I was unaware of its depth and ramifications. For instance, I was not prepared to encounter outright hatred of the aged on the Internet. More than one posting made it quite clear what the writer wanted: "Get out of the way, you . . . old bastards, and the sooner the better!" Such sentiment may come as a surprise to many readers, and it took me a while to confront the painful fact that writers of this type express openly what many others really think, though they would likely not subscribe to the crude animus of "flaming" scribblers and therefore choose to guard their tongues—or their fingers. Whenever I come across this kind of sentiment I think of Evelyn Waugh's remark: "As a matter of fact, elderly people are not more contemptible than anyone else."

In my own pastoral work I have seen more than a few old people shunned by their own families, a sad fact borne out by a French scholar:

In hospices and hospitals the number of old people who die without having received even a fleeting visit from their relatives is growing. In France, according to recent data, this state of affairs has now reached the incredible figure of 60% of deaths at nursing homes for the elderly.

Why? Because the old remind others of the road they themselves will have to travel. They therefore see us as representing death-in-waiting, and they do not like it.

Don't Show Your Age

"Old" used to be a word with overtones of "good value." Thus, an old hat was something of a cherished possession; today it is a likely candidate for the Goodwill store, and the expression "old hat" has the sense of something that once was probably newsworthy and even worthwhile but is now passé. That is but one example of many. With a few exceptions, "old" has become something of dubious worth; hence, people tend to avoid the term when speaking of other people. They do not want to be politically incorrect or inadvertently imply the wrong message. Just saying "old" about anything or anyone can get them into trouble.

In certain combinations the term continues to mean the same as it did a hundred years ago. An "old friend" is someone we have known for a long time, someone who makes us feel good. In the eighteenth century, Oliver Goldsmith could still write: "I love everything that's old: old friends, old times, old manners, old books, old wine." As regards friends and wine this perception remains intact, but the rest does not. Old times are more often forgotten than remembered, old-fashioned attitudes are irrelevant, and old books are for a minority in love with the past. Most people look for the new. A house will be hard to sell in the year 2000 if it is said to be old, while a hundred years ago its age might likely have been an attraction. The laptop computer on which this book is being written, having served me for five or six years, is considered old. While still useful to me, it has become quite unsaleable (and therefore less likely to be stolen when I leave it unguarded in a hotel room).

That, of course, is no surprise when it comes to products in a constantly changing technological environment. But how about people? Alas, while old people used to be admired (and in some cultures still are), they are now more like things that have lost their worth and been left behind by time. California philosopher Joseph L. Esposito therefore calls aging "the beginning of social extinction, the time when an individual becomes obsolete as an active member of bustling society."

Look at your newspaper or listen to radio and TV, and you will hardly find anyone saying that a certain person is "old." Maybe "elderly"— but "old"? No, that would be a serious faux pas.

This linguistic blip occasions the strange fact that while more people get older, no one seems to become "old." No wonder people are frightened when grey hair is sneaking up on them and wonder whether techniques like coloring, face-lifting, skin-smoothing, wearing wigs or other methods can postpone the day when others will discover the real person underneath the fake cover.

Not long ago only women were said to be trying to hide their age; now men are just as eager to be considered younger than they are. True, this development is not something totally new. Two hundred years ago Western men used to wear peruques, probably to conceal their balding pates, and an ancient folk tale speculates that the biblical Joseph helped his good looks along by curling his eyelashes and painting his eyebrows. Fashions tend to come in cycles, revealing something of the way society sees itself. Here is how a first-century Roman writer perceived this tendency: "When you try to conceal your wrinkles, Polla, with paste made from beans, you deceive yourself, not me."

It is noteworthy that the word "make-up" describes both the stuff people apply to their faces and the deception they practice by making something up that is not really so. It is easier for everyone to play the game and pretend that "old" applies to no one, certainly no one we know. Who would want to call another person over-the-hill and useless? And if you ask, "When is it permissible to say it as it is?" the answer might be: "Maybe some day, but not now."

All of which is an expression of what has lately been called "ageism," defined by the inventor of the word as "a deep-seated uneasiness on the part of the young and middle-aged—a personal revulsion to and distaste for growing old, disease and disability, and fear of powerlessness, 'uselessness' and death."

How has this come about? Why are antiques prized because they are old, while people are not and therefore dare not be so identified lest they be abandoned as worthless? Perhaps it has to do with the remarkable achievements of modern medicine. It holds out the promise to cure us of our diseases and to postpone the day of death for a long and ever longer time. Of course, we know that everyone, including you and me, has to die. But not for a while—and who knows, perhaps a long while. Why then remind us of approaching death by calling us "old"? No wonder that in the United States, Grandparents Day (celebrated in September) has not yet made it into public consciousness and remains widely unobserved.

Words Can Be Daggers

It is not only what people actually do to their elders, it is also the way they talk about them that shows how the old are regarded. A monograph entitled *The Semiotics of Ageism* has even put together a little dictionary of "ageist" terms. Here are some samples:

Ageist nouns: bag, battle ax, biddy, codger, coot, crone, decrepitude, fogey, fuddy-duddy, geezer, goat, hag, little old lady, old timer, old woman (referring to a timid man), second childhood, senility, spinster, old maid, old wives' tale, witch. The latest addition to this catalogue is "no-neck"; heard in Florida, it is used for older drivers not tall enough for their heads to be seen clearly above the steering wheel of a car.

Ageist adjectives: crotchety, doddering, grumpy, infirm, superannuated, toothless, withered, wizened, wrinkled.

Of course, some of these words are perfectly acceptable in a neutral context, but when describing older people they become ageist terms. Sometimes gender prejudice compounds the offense; for example, "showing one's age" refers usually to a woman's normal aging process and has a negative meaning, and many of the above-listed terms are also sexist.

Positive terms exist as well, especially when applied to geographic or political entities, such as Old Glory (the United States flag) and Old Faithful (a famous Yellowstone geyser); but they do also occasionally function as endearments, as in "old friend" or "old fellow." Other terms strike a positive or at least neutral tone: experienced, mature, mellow, sage, seasoned, veteran, well versed, wise, old hand. "Elder" is pretty safe from verbal abuse, but "alderman" (elder man), seen as sexist, is not. "Generation gap" used to be an objective description of age difference when it was first used (in the sixties), but it quickly became a put-down, suggesting that the older party lacked a proper understanding of the young.

"Discrimination" is a word usually applied to minority problems, and in that sense we oldsters too could be called a minority, though that ascription has so far not been applied to us. The problem is confounded by the fact that prejudicial terms can be found not only in the media but also in children's books and school texts. We have been reasonably successful in cleansing our language of racist epithets, and geographic or national or identifications like "newfie" (someone from Newfoundland) or "polack" are no longer acceptable, but no comparable effort has been made to alert decent folk about the pernicious effect of using ageist terms. It is time we tried. Some publications have plowed the ground for it, and they deserve wider recognition. A social critic puts it pithily: "Growing old in today's fragmented, age-phobic, age-segregated America is to inhabit a foreign country, isolated, disconnected, and misunderstood."

We oldsters are quite unwilling to be cast on the societal ash heap as unusable antiques and be talked about accordingly. We may agree in our hearts that things have gone downhill in some respects, but we would like people to play the right language card when talking about us. As noted, there are acceptable terms for those of us who have passed the 65-year mark, though there is every likelihood that tomorrow they will acquire the flavor of "seniors"—which was acceptable yesterday but has become infected with ageism. "Super seniors," as the oldest category in tennis tournaments is known, is still an accolade rather than a verbal sneer, while "golden age" is no longer acceptable and joins the category of apparently neutral terms that often become cover words for prejudice. Besides, the term also hides an unpleasant reality. For all too many, the years are rarely good enough to be called golden. And even those of us who are okay in most respects find ourselves in a situation that threatens to become more difficult .

The reader may wonder whether any term that describes us who are chronologically old is really neutral and immune from becoming discriminatory. Probably not, as long as society views the old as "over the hill" and wishes them out of the way. I would like to help rescue the word "old" from its current negative habitat and, more important, put my aging contemporaries into a more respectable social light and thereby give them a heightened sense of self-respect. A bit ambitious, but then, being old does not have to mean you lose your ambition.

The famous lines from Robert Browning that were once so popular are nowadays heard but rarely, even though our life span has expanded miraculously:

Grow old along with me!
The best is yet to be,
The last of life,
For which the first was made . . .

It would help if society would learn this stanza, take it to heart, and act on it. For the time being, however, its perception is different.

I Should Be Young, Not Old

Memories of a Vanished Culture

Youth has always conjured up images of nostalgic pleasure—seen through the eyes of aging adults, anyway. Falling in love was primarily the privilege of young people, who by definition possessed wide-eyed innocence, smooth skin, and enormous physical and emotional energy. Romantic literature considered the last as superior to the exercise of reason, which was the domain of mature people.

The start of modernity is usually traced to the romanticism of the late eighteenth century. A few generations later that movement was pushed aside by Victorian strictures, which in their day were considered politically correct (though the term did not yet exist). But some inveterate romantics like Gustave Flaubert disregarded the rules by writing about older people behaving like young kids—falling in love—and about women as aged as thirty-something having affairs with younger men, something that the author's critics were wont to characterize as perverse. Victorian sentiment persisted into the twentieth century. My wife remembers how, when she was in her teens and went to dances in Cincinnati, she once saw some people past thirty on the dance floor and thought it to be bordering on indecency. The young had their place and so did "old" folks, and the latter too had to abide by the rules.

I grew up in Germany, where youth movements were just beginning to question Victorian values and advocate a return to the nature-oriented romanticism of the past. They demanded their place in the sun, but my parents paid no attention to them when they brought us up. My brother and I were to be seen at the table and not to be heard unless spoken to. Obedience was expected from us, and teachers were allowed to slap their students without incurring the wrath of the law—on the contrary, physical punishment was deemed to be the most effective means of controlling their charges. "Spare the rod and spoil the child" was Samuel Butler's oft cited warning, considered to be a proper interpretation of the biblical verse, "Discipline your child, for only then is there any hope, but do not overdo it."

My parents were probably an exception in that they instilled discipline in my brother and me without resorting to physical force of any kind. The one time I was hit therefore became a traumatic experience. It happened during the First World War, when I was four or five years old. Mother had cultivated a tiny patch of ground behind our apartment building in Berlin and was raising tomatoes, a fruit that was then quite rare, to supplement our sparse diet. One day, for whatever reason, I knocked the ripening fruit off the stalks, thereby finishing off Mother's experiment in nutritional supplements. Her anger and my surprise at her slapping my face had a lasting effect on me. Well into my married years I thoroughly disliked tomatoes, until I traced my distaste back to the slap they caused me during the Great War. Dad would probably not have reacted like Mother, for he was a softy and, as father and pedagogue, very different from his colleagues—especially from my math teacher, whose left-handedness I still remember. I encountered his physical preference one day when he asked me a question I could not answer right away. He was walking up and down the aisle, which I found quite unthreatening because I sat to the left of him, and was therefore shocked when, with the back of his left hand, he suddenly cuffed me in order to awaken my intellect and fear—and he certainly achieved the latter objective.

I recall the time I first encountered a 17th-century painting that, depicting a boy, showed him not as a youth but as a little man. At that time such a way of expressing reality was quite common, for children were perceived as adults in the making and had not yet been given their own distinctive personalities. A hundred years later, Gainsborough's "Blue Boy" was a boy, all right, and looked like one. But seen from today's perspective it is the older artists who relate to our age, for we treat young people as adults to be. Physical punishment of a child by a parent is now considered an interference with the latter's normal growth and could engender a charge of criminal assault. One may speculate just why this shift of perceptions seems to emulate an earlier period of human history, at least in a painterly way, and that it happened only a generation ago.

The Sixties Revolution

More and more people now begin to recognize that not only the former Soviet empire but also the Western world underwent a dramatic reshaping in the fairly immediate past. I do not refer to the globalization of information that made a thirty-year-old the richest man in the world but to the sociopsychological events that started during the 1960s and continue unabated today .

The crux of this veritable revolution was not the popularization of mind-enhancing substances, which attracted public attention, but the rediscovery of romanticism. Only this time it was not confined to the realm of literature and the arts. The core change manifested itself first in youthful gatherings all over North America, during which the participants by their behavior demonstrated their disdain for accepted parental restraints (also dubbed bourgeois or Victorian) and made bold to rewrite the rules of interpersonal values. They opposed the Vietnam conflict, called for love instead of war, shed formal modes of dress, and announced a shift of priorities. They were the baby boomers, who at first stressed community but then proceeded to emphasize individuality. In the beginning they said "Me too" and then "Me first," and demanded their place in the sun right then and there.

One of the lasting effects of their arrival on the scene was the growing perception that the past no longer mattered and only the new knowledge of love and technology had significance. Henry Ford was thus crowned with posthumous laurels, for he had proclaimed a long time ago that "history is bunk." In the days of the Second World War and the fifties, history had been the number one subject in school. No more, the sciences have taken its place.

(An aside: even a lot of Israelis, though living in the land of historical memory, are increasingly uninterested in history. In the spring of 1998 the fiftieth anniversary celebrations of the state did not evoke as deep an emotional response in the young as one might have expected. Israel's secular youth have for some years evinced their preference for a Western mindset and many of them, like their North American models, are not convinced that even fundamental events like the Holocaust continue to have relevance for them. The Shoah and its six million victims belong to the past, these youngsters think, and the past is dying out or already dead. They have little or no need for it.)

It strikes me as the ultimate irony that the very boomers who liberated themselves from the older folk are now getting their come-uppance in spades. Their youngsters not only criticize them as elders (which is all right), but also declare their past irrelevant (which is painful; the boomers never went that far). A seventeen-year-old's essay, prominently published by Canada's best known newspaper, was headlined "Brave new world of teen autonomy" and proclaimed:

> Teen-agers today are influenced by other teen-agers, television, celebrity endorsements, music, gang standards. Not by adults, whose importance in our lives has plummeted to an all-time low.

The same theme was explored in a recent, highly controversial book. Judith Rich Harris questions the accepted belief that the home is the most important factor in forming a child's character. The young person's peers, she says, play an even more important role in this respect, usually eclipsing the influence of the parents. Our children's friends, Ms. Harris claims, account for more than what we try to teach at home. Which means that even in bringing up our offspring we yield our major function to other youth. Parents, and even more so grandparents, have thus been relegated to the margin of children's lives.

How the Media Treat Us

From such building blocks has emerged the edifice we occupy today, the house that information built. Browsing the Internet is to a large extent the domain of the young, who have vastly more knowledge in this area than older people. Fashion ads direct themselves primarily to the young; the fact that many feature anorexic images rather than believable people fits right in with this trend. Emaciated women are expected to look like teenagers rather than adults. These creatures are the offspring of the youth culture. And why women? Because the surfers, hackers, and other browsers are mostly boys who look less for knowledge (of which they believe they already have a surfeit) than for entertainment. They find lots of it there, enough to engage them for hours at a time, wandering the byways of the net, where all too often they encounter violence and sex—at a time in their lives when their technical skills exceed their emotional capacities.

We aged folk are supposed to know nothing about any of this. We are by definition on the road to senility, which the *American Heritage Dictionary* defines *inter alia* as "mental and physical deterioration with old age." It reflects the kind of view that, like all prejudice, is hard to fight. We are thought of as potential victims of Alzheimer's disease or other forms of dementia, tottering along life's highway until we fall into our final ditch. The computer industry, which is the most innovative branch of modern business, seems only dimly aware of our presence and, surprisingly, underestimates our buying power. We are largely overlooked as consumers of electronic products, despite the fact that a lot of us are in fact connected to the net and generally have time to look around. For some reason we do not interest the purveyors of either electronic or print media, except to sell us condos in sun cities, devices for locomotion, penile erections, and other goodies that we are believed to need or crave and that are advertised primarily in specialty publications of the AARP and CARP, the two major North American organizations of retired persons. This despite the fact that a significant segment of the readership of all print media consists of the aging public. No one has described this imbalance more graphically than Carolyn Heilbrun:

> Except in advertisements of dentifrices designed for the wearers of false teeth, or laxatives to rescue the aging from their consti-

pation, the young dominate the airwaves, television, the fashion ads, the Internet (and the technology to access it), and the movies. The aging, while nervous about HMOs, Medicare, and Social Security, do not seem to play a very large role in this country's affairs—aging women even less than men.

Television too rarely portrays the old in either programs or ads. A sampling of ads that do use aging people, includes a sixty-year-old woman hitting a golf ball, exclaiming, "It's never too late" (to strengthen your bones by using the advertised calcium product); grandpa gently refusing the marriage proposal of his little granddaughter and proving withal that he has still enough oomph to push her bike—if he eats the right kind of dietary supplement; Joe and Jane, presumably on in years, walking off hand in hand toward the setting sun (message: they would love to hear from you by telephone before their sun goes down permanently); and my least favorite: the proverbial little old lady in tennis shoes. She comes into a showroom to buy a car. Instead of the salesperson asking what model she has in mind or what price range, this one goes right to the perceived heart of the matter and says: "Very good, Ma'am, what color do you like?" And when he shows her the car she looks at it, kicks the tire, and proclaims convincingly (so the ad hopes) that this sedan is the automobile of choice for people like her.

Grumpy Old Men is the telling title of a film featuring two friends who both conspire and fight with each other, and while it is often funny it is also ageist. The very fact that they are old is supposed to give the production a special humorous twist. It is one thing when friends quarrel, and it's funny when the two are old.

The major exception I have found is a British half-hour sitcom. Called *Waiting for God*, it features two old-timers, Diana Trent and Tom Ballard, who live in a retirement complex run by a self-important manager who knows his charges as budget items rather than as live persons. Diana is the one who tells it as it is, calling herself old, entitled to live life as fully as she can, which includes satisfying her sexual impulses—whether or not others around her like it (the oldsters like it, the younger ones do not). In outrageous punch lines of fine-tuned English, she rants at the injustice visited on the old by their younger "prison keepers," and in the defense of her perceived rights she does not care whom she offends. All people in this comedy of old life are depicted as caricatures, and the laughs are many—a rare treat in the usual somber recital of the problems of old age. (Besides, Diana and Tom usually win, which in real life they would not likely accomplish.)

Humor does in fact give the old a chance to be heard on occasion. Outstanding among aging comedians was George Burns, who made his advanced years (he died a centenarian) a platform for his one-liners. TV and films made him the outstanding exception in an arena that the aged rarely entered. When someone asked him why he never was without a cigar, he answered: "Because at my age, I'd fall down if I didn't have something to hold onto." And, when asked what restrictions old age had imposed upon him, he said: "I don't buy green bananas any more."

Films have occasionally done a little better. *On Golden Pond* presented the tale of two aging people, and was not patronizing in either title or story line. *Golden* was of course an allusion to "golden age," on which I commented earlier; "pond" struck me as a peaceful little self-contained body of water—a metaphor of old age.

Though books are not "media" in the accepted sense, I must mention the incomparable Dr. Seuss, who, in his 83rd year, wrote and illustrated *You're Only Old Once: A Book for Obsolete Children*. It is a journey through the jungle of a medical clinic where doctors "ogle" and nurse Becker "becks" the patient when the doc is ready. I read it as a geriatric update of Charlie Chaplin's *Modern Times*, albeit cast in a much narrower frame, wherein the old stand for dignity amid our troubles, hoping that we readers will be "in pretty good shape for the shape [we] are in." Like Mother Goose rhymes, the book is aimed at adults, and its universal appeal lies in the fact that its words and drawings are vintage Seuss, so that children too not only love it but think it was meant for them.

In sum, there is lots of room for the old to be heard and seen more often, in roles and plots that give them the kind of dignity that is so often denied them. Meanwhile, the young will continue to dominate the screens at home and in the theaters. Maybe there will be changes when the baby boomers join the army of the old and will start asserting themselves. That will be a good day for everyone.

Young Is Good, Old Is Bad

Meanwhile, the glorification of the young has sunk deep roots into our culture, to the detriment of both young and old. Not surprisingly, the young relish the spotlight, the adulation, and the acclaim of the middle-aged crowd who pretend that somehow they too can recover a portion of their past. "Keep young," the ads shout at them, "Watch your vitamins," "Get your exercise," "Don't carry extra pounds" (which already the teenagers interpret to mean that it is better to be anorexic or bulimic than to be overweight).

There used to be a popular quip that proclaimed, "Better to be rich and healthy than to be poor and sick." The low-key wit conveyed by this banality lay in the way the obvious was expressed, for everyone knows that there is no premium on illness or poverty.

But a new version has sprung up, and it goes like this: "Better to be young and rich than to be old and poor." While the rich/poor contrast is still there, the healthy/sick one has been replaced. "Healthy" is now identified with young, and "sick" with old. The shift is subtle and most people smile when they hear it. I do not. For wit, however flat, often reflects the real feelings people have about life. To be sure, as we age we become more susceptible to illness, and in that sense all aging is debility in the making. But to pronounce this potential to be our chief characteristic is just one more way of stereotyping us and shoving us into the category of incompetence, uselessness, and low cost-effectiveness. When you combine these supposed deficiencies we are, literally, no joke.

In the province of Ontario, where I live, the government has introduced a rule that people over eighty must prove themselves to be competent if they want to keep on driving their cars. Similar arrangements exist in some American jurisdictions. I have written elsewhere about my experience with this badly administered and ill thought-out law and will not do so here.

Insurance companies would, of course, be the first to target us oldsters and charge us increased premiums, but they do not. Why? A major reason is that we voluntarily restrict our driving when we (or our families) feel that we no longer want to fight our way through traffic. In consequence, carefully constructed actuarial tables show the insurers that we do not represent a special risk. They do sock it to male drivers under the age of twenty-five, but not to us. Still, as so often, governments know better. "Get off the road," they tell us without embarrassment. Just as they see us as a drain on the public purse, so they consider us a danger to others when we are behind the wheel. The public, if polled, would probably agree, for it regurgitates the pap it is fed by our culture and its spokespeople. So, leave the road to the young. They know how to drive at 60 miles per hour in a 30-mile-per-hour zone, zipping and weaving in and out without indicating lane changes. Even when dangerous they are admired.

There is a lesson in this mismanaged matter. Because we old-timers were not as quiet as we were supposed to be and mounted a public counter-offensive (that I kicked off with an article in the Toronto *Globe & Mail*), the bureaucrats yielded some ground and made changes in this demeaning procedure. Grey power can make itself felt if we get off our seats and use it.

The heart of our social problem is that society treats us as obsolete and thereby marks us as essentially worthless (though costly). Art Linkletter is supposed to have described the four stages of life as infancy, childhood, prolonged adolescence, and obsolescence.

Of course, we are no longer the cultural treasures we once were, functioning as transmitters of history to the next generation. Not only is that gone, but the process has been reversed: The young now have the information (if not the knowledge), while the old are envious. Since "old" has become a synonym for passé, "new" stands for "good" or "better." Advertisements often do not bother to tell us why a new gadget is superior to the old; it seems sufficient to inform the public that it is new, and therefore by definition improved.

I once read that mystery writer Agatha Christie's second husband was an archeologist, and that when asked what it was like being married to a man with such interests, she was said to have answered: "It's great; the older I get the more interested he is in me." The fact is that a lot of oldsters are indeed more interesting than their younger contemporaries, though our society does not see it that way.

The sixties revolution is not the only culprit in this development. It is also part of the fall-out from the economic system that fuels our prosperity, a system that is based on two complementary principles:

1) Rapid technological advance will produce ever-newer products that are superior to the old, and consumers are therefore urged to replace them.

2) Since products will be obsolete after a short time there is no point in making them durable, and consequently built-in obsolescence is part of their manufacture.

This background of our contemporary economic structure is not often mentioned, because people have a natural desire to preserve what they have and are not keen on contemplating the fact that the item on which they spend their hard earned cash will in a few years be destined for obsolescence. Hence they pretend or piously believe that their purchase will last, although deep down they know it will not. This is another aspect of the "Don't call anyone old" syndrome.

Everyone knows that economic values influence our culture, so that the obsolescence of goods casts a shadow over the durability of everything, including people and their relationships. Lifelong jobs are becoming a thing of the past, lifelong marriages have become fewer, and old people are seen as obsolete, just like things in the marketplace. No one admits it candidly, for—as I have said repeatedly and will say again—we old people are rarely a fit subject for public discussion.

No wonder the second space flight of 77-year-old John Glenn electrified the elder population and gave the *Discovery* takeoff in November 1998 a special dimension. I was in the States at the time and joined in the excitement. Wherever I turned, the older crowd felt that Glenn was doing it for them as well. One reporter wrote of a woman, 76 years of age, who wiped away a tear and said: "Maybe now young people will look differently at us. We're not just old. We're not useless. We can contribute to the world." Dr. Gene Cohen, a geriatric psychiatrist at George Washington University, called the astronaut's exploit "a wonderful example of the creative interplay of mind and body." For once the media joined in and took the oldsters' side (over the objections by some who considered the whole thing a publicity stunt at the expense of the taxpayer), agreeing that there was a legitimate objective to Glenn's participation: Why do all astronauts exposed to zero gravity experience a kind of bone loss resembling that seen in the aging process, and how did Glenn fare in comparison to his colleagues? Perhaps by the time this book appears the results will be known.

For some as yet unexamined reason, orchestra conductors, artists, and writers remain productive in their advanced years. Toscanini, Picasso, and Goethe are examples that readily come to mind. Another is architect Frank Lloyd Wright, who, ending a long dry spell, started building his most imaginative structures (among them the Guggenheim Museum on New York's Fifth Avenue) after reaching the eighty-year mark. No fewer than twenty-one established artists announced their boycott of the museum when the drawings for it first became public, but Wright battled them and other doubters like a young bullfighter, and prevailed. Unfortunately he died just a few months before the Guggenheim was finished. He was 92 years old.

Not all Western countries have imitated the North American tendency to see aging as a dubious contribution to the common weal. An illustrated calendar issued by the German federal government shows four seniors as part of a rowing team. The sidebar reads:

> Old, but not idle. Rising longevity has placed the generation of our pensioners into the center of national life. They are active participants in Project Witnesses to History, which is now part of the school curriculum. They dialogue with the young and tell them of Germany's past. Business enterprises too take advantage of the counsel that our elders can give. In 1999, Germany will try to do justice to the celebration of the "International Year of Older Persons."

A personal afterthought: I do not hanker to be young again. My youth, with its many problems and agonies, is not something I would wish to repeat. I say this only to remind the reader that stereotypes seldom lead anywhere except into dead-end alleys.

There is much talk about the social issues deriving from the explosive increase of the geriatric population, but how we oldsters feel about being caught in this highly publicized squeeze play is apparently not fit for discussion.

People Like Me
Are Causing Problems

Unprecedented Longevity

In the spring of 1998, the Director General of the World Health Organization (WHO) issued a report on global aging, entitled *Life in the 21st Century: A Vision for All*. Its figures are startling. Even though we are all aware that longevity has increased and will increase further, its rise has been nothing short of dramatic.

In the days of ancient Greece, the average longevity was 30 years, and if people lived to 60 they were considered old. This knowledge is garnered from classic literature, for statistics in the modern sense were unknown. Had there been a survey of the next two thousand years, it would have shown little increase or decrease, with the latter occurring in times of war, famine, and epidemics (like the medieval Black Plague) or their absence.

Not until the beginning of the twentieth century did statistics show a notable change, and from then on the numbers kept on rising, slowly at first and in the last few decades ever more rapidly.

Just how many of us are there today? Of course, any figures become out of date the moment they are set down in print—but the trend speaks volumes (showing North American figures as examples):

Since 1900, the percentage of persons 65 or older has more than tripled. The 65–74 age group is eight times larger than it was in 1900; the 75–84 group is 16 times larger; and the 85 and up segment 31 times larger. And among the last, centenarians are increasing the fastest. The trend shows no sign of halting, let alone of reversing itself. By 2030, the projection shows, there will be about seventy million older persons, more than twice the number we have today.

A whole variety of factors are now identified as determining a person's longevity: genetic and biological background, ecology, social environment, nutrition, physical activities, hygiene, preventive medicine, personality, intelligence, adaptation, mental activity, and finally, a sense of humor. In most societies, the educated and well-to-do have a greater chance of living longer than the uneducated and poor. Hence, figures for industrialized countries show greater longevity than those for the Third World. We in the West will probably have the largest numbers of old people to live with, support, and look after.

In addition, more people are aiming for and reaching the 100-year mark and can obtain advice on how to get there and, when they do, how to handle what is left of their life.

Too Many Oldsters?

The consequences of this spectacular growth are multiple. They have to do with health care, insurance, poverty, age discrimination, and a host of other issues. Some of them are economic, others cultural, and all of them are part psychological and part physiological.

A famous saying comes to my mind. At one point in Egypt's history the pharaoh took a look at his slave population, among whom the Israelites constituted a fair percentage. Said he: "Look here, these Israelites are becoming too many for us, so let us make workable plans to deal with their increase, for if we do not and get into a war, they may rise up and join the enemy."

We old people are the new Israelites: Like them, we are perceived as becoming too many and thereby creating a problem not only to society but to ourselves as well. Contrary to the prejudicial fascination of the media with inhabitants of nursing homes, only a small percentage (perhaps as low as 4 percent) of old people reside in them, while most of us live normally integrated lives—living in a family environment, alone or in a group facility. To be sure, some media focus on nursing homes is legitimate and, in fact, necessary when certain shortcomings of institutional care are being exposed.

There is, however, no question that the explosive increase of the geriatric population has brought in its train certain social problems. Forecasters paint the economic and other consequences in the darkest colors, but how we oldsters feel about being caught in this highly publicized squeeze play is apparently not fit for discussion. The blunt truth is that we are being blamed for having lived so long and demanding too much, thereby upsetting the economic scales of society.

After all, citizens pay into a savings program and expect to get the accumulated funds back when the agreed-upon terms are fulfilled, hoping that the interest and perhaps other accretions will provide them with a decent nest egg. The most famous of these programs is the Social Security system of the United States. Introduced in the nineteen-thirties by Franklin D. Roosevelt, it was a copy of a political master-stroke by German Chancellor Otto von Bismarck fifty years before. (Actually, Thomas Paine had already suggested such a scheme in the late 18th century, but his pamphlet had long been forgotten.) Lately, the U.S. program is constantly in the news, because of the increasing fear that there will not be enough money left for tomorrow's retirees, which renders the "security" of Social Security an illusion. I have a seen a good deal of finger-pointing on the Internet, the American Association of Retired Persons (AARP) being targeted for draining the national coffers on behalf of its members. Of course this accusation contains a grain of truth. For the AARP and in Canada, CARP, do encourage my contemporaries to keep on living and thereby driving the longevity curve right off the charts.

When the social safety net was instituted during the Great Depression, the population pyramid had the old-fashioned shape: It was broad at the base, with the young being the largest segment, while the top (the prospective retirees) consisted of relatively few people. The broad base included the wage earners who paid into the fund, while the few at the pinnacle collected their modest share. The feared-for future sees the pyramid standing on its head: too few paying into the fund, and too many getting paid. Despite all assurances by the politicians, the baby boomers and their children remain skeptical, fearing that even if they pay an even more substantial amount into the system they will not be able to collect when their time comes. No wonder they have begun to think about it all as a social insecurity system. In Canada, the government issued me a special plastic reminder of my future when I turned 65. My new identity card features Parliament at night, with only a few lights still on. I got the message.

The problem is complicated by the fact that a lot of boomers are used to changing their careers and would rather continue working at a different job than retire altogether. They need employment because they still feel young enough and also because their retirement income may be insufficient to keep them from eventually sliding into poverty. Highlighting this trend is a book tellingly called *UnRetirement*, which identifies employers' myths about aging as a chief hindrance to sensible hiring practices; it also stresses the contribution that this generation has made to society and wants to keep on making without interference from a public mired in social stereotypes. The boomers have controlled their lives so far, but when they want to manage their future they may meet the same obstacles that barred their elders' way to equitable treatment.

In any case, it is likely that the 65-year marker for retirement will give way to a 68- or 70-year figure in the years to come. And the moment that occurs, the pressure will be on to raise the marker even further, so that more years of productive living may lie ahead of an aging population.

From Prejudice to Obsolescence

Nothing in human relationships remains a one-way street. Economic obsolescence helps to create "obsolete" people, and the increasing numbers of the latter affect economic developments. To put it simply and starkly: The older employees get (especially once they pass the half-century mark), the greater the threat that they will lose their jobs before they reach retirement. They may possess a wealth of experience, which formerly was highly prized, but they are also becoming more and more expensive to employ. Our cultural environment suggests that younger people would not only be cheaper but also do better (which is one of the above-noted fables). They are seen as having more energy and ambition and as incurring fewer absences because of illness. More and more employers have therefore reached the conclusion that the simplest solution is to let the older workers go. The practice has been threatening to spread so rapidly that the affected groups and social libertarians managed to introduce restraining laws. In Canada, at least, more equitable trends have emerged in middle-size companies. Yet the Supreme Court of the country has ruled that age discrimination is not illegal when the victims are over 65.

In the 1980s and early 1990s, I sat as an adjudicator (in effect, an *ad hoc* judge) in human rights court, and cases alleging age discrimination were beginning to increase. In those days it was still possible to discern the economic intent of employers, but since then they have become more sophisticated and hide it behind "justifiable economic interests," as they have lately called their excuses. Downsizing is the newest screen behind which age discrimination often lurks. In 1987, a U.S. Court of Appeals ruled that cost cutting was not a legitimate, non-discriminatory reason for discharging an older employee while retaining younger employees paid at a lower scale. "Yet every year," said one report on the Web, "thousands and thousands of U.S. workers are quietly downsized, demoted or somehow discriminated against on the job for one reason only: because they are getting older."

As I can tell from my own judicial experience, age discrimination is not always provable and in a given case may in fact not at all have been the reason for the employee's discharge. But it does exist and the aging employee fears it. The potential offenders are not necessarily found only in the private sector; public bodies are not exempt from the temptation of using questionable means of "saving the taxpayers money," as such practices are piously called. Thus, teachers are known to stay at their jobs until they are ready for retirement, and by the time they reach that time in their life they are likely at the top of their earning schedule. Younger teachers cost much less.

In Ontario, age discrimination is a legal offense only when the offended party is between 18 and 64 years old. When prospective employers say to a 23-year old, "You are too young for this kind of job," or to a 63-year-old, "You are too old," they have violated the Ontario Human Rights Code. Similar legislative provisions obtain throughout North America. But someone 65 or over can be the target of undisguised and perfectly legal discrimination. Never mind the injured self-worth of the rejected person. He or she may have earned the Nobel Prize for some wonderful recent contribution to humanity, but to the law the laureate is obsolete. That law is an ass.

Related problems that rarely have legal implications also play their role. While one of the basic rules of medical care is human equality (that is, all sick people have a claim on treatment), community resources are often strained, and some people will be looked after while others are not, or not adequately. Choices are made on a variety of grounds, among which age plays a significant role. Doctors and institutions thus would find themselves faced with the old ethical problem.

It achieved prominence during the First World War, when trench warfare turned to mass slaughter and French army doctors in field hospitals had to sort out whom to treat first. Injured men who had a chance of surviving were given preference, while those with little chance of making it were left to die. This terrible task of sorting (French *trier*) became known as triage. Modern hospitals practice it today when faced with a large-scale emergency; nurses may practice it (de facto triage) when they are overworked and cannot possibly serve all patients adequately. In circumstances of this kind aged folk are likely to be the last to receive treatment. In California, a doctor told me recently that in the emergency room they have a name for an older man who is put at the end of the line. They call him a "gomer"—an acronym for "grand old man in emergency room" or "get out of my emergency room."

Where Shall We Go?

Until hospitals and related places of care came into existence, most of the aged lived and died in the midst of their narrow or extended families. Both suffering and death were accepted as ineluctable aspects of living. Though lots of families probably had trouble accommodating the old, there were no alternatives, and they felt morally obligated to do what they could. The problems that arose found expression in a medieval Jewish saying, that grandmothers are a blessing to one's home, while grandfathers are a pain in the neck. I take this to reflect a woman's continued willingness to perform household tasks and a man's lack of interest in such matters, coupled nonetheless with a demand for attention and authority.

Today of course, we have homes for the aged, hospitals of many kinds, nursing homes and similar places where permanent or temporary incapacity (of the patient or the caregiver) is tended to. They range from very good to very bad, depending on a multitude of factors, among which profit, availability of funds and community support are decisive.. One reads of ghastly abuse of patients as well as of loving care. Fortunately, there are today a multitude of retirement homes or complexes, where living in a protected environment and in a community are major attractions. Lately, a novel communal arrangement is finding favor. Called "assisted living," it provides needed health services, meals, companionship, and watchful care, while keeping the elderly in their own homes.

A critical exploration of institutional care exceeds the limits of this book. As always, the more money people have, the more options exist and the more variety is available. The media are filled with tempting images of picturesque communities or developments where golf, tennis, and other activities beckon potential customers. These are the preferred retreats of the financially comfortable, offering a good climate and enough of a variety of social opportunities to ward off the deadly virus of boredom, and providing pleasurable exercise and other ways of keeping mind and body companionable. It is the kind of environment in which getting old is an acceptable subject of conversation, since everyone is in the same boat. But even at the best of times, only a relatively small percentage of the aging population will be able to afford such choices.

The advantages of these retreats for the aged are self-evident. To a goodly degree they make it possible for their inhabitants-whether for part of the time or all year round—to leave the rejectionist climate of ordinary society for the balmy weather of mutual acceptance. Here too are drawbacks, however, for younger generations are not part of the scene. I know of one self-contained city of and for the old, where the minimum age of admission is 55. Younger faces are seen now and then, when relatives come for a visit—an arrangement which amounts to reverse age discrimination, possibly tinged with subconscious sentiments of revenge. Thus, one can buy a large chunk of satisfaction with money, but never the whole thing.

Since the majority cannot begin to afford such luxuries, they are forced to endure the slings and arrows of general society, with its negative feeling toward the old and are thus thrust back on their own familial, economic and emotional resources. Increasingly, many look to gambling casinos, which raise their hopes but drain their pockets. Ah, but for life's lacking fairness!

Not Every Problem Has a Solution

The North American hospice program was born out of a specific dilemma posed by people with cancer and other terminal diseases. Facing death is hard for anyone, but facing it alone is terrifying. Giving companionship, lending a willing ear, and offering a sense of compassion are powerful antidotes to despair. Before "hospice" became a common word of hope, suicides among the old were more numerous than those of teenagers. Everyone talked of the latter, while the former attracted little public attention. The young seemed to have options and had only to recognize them, while the aged appeared to have none left. The hospice movement has shown that friendship and honesty can replace the growing dread of life's last days and months with a feeling of peace and dignity. Its main features have been well summarized in this fashion:

- Honoring of patients' wishes whenever possible.
- Comfort care (keeping patients free of pain and discomfort).
- More than medical help (assisting patients with spiritual, emotional, and everyday practical needs).
- Family involvement, including counseling its members before and after the patient's death.
- Counseling and assistance for care givers in their often arduous task.
- Teamwork (combining a panoply of professionals with volunteers).

These programs also include care in people's own homes—and for the patient, that is often by far the most salutary way of maintaining a sense of belonging. Still, hospice is not for everyone; people have different needs. "Some may prefer quantity over quality—like many of the 414 hospital patients 80 and older who participated in a recent University of Cincinnati Medical Center study. They said that they'd rather live longer in their current state of health than live a shorter life in better health." Compassionate attention helps the old benefit along with everyone else, and happily, such programs are now found in all good homes for the aged and similar places where expecting the end of the journey is part of the scene.

I should add a word about hastening the end. At best, statistics dealing with prematurely induced deaths are unreliable, for it is certain that they are not regularly reported. Public debates rage around assisted suicide, with one American doctor, Jack Kevorkian, advocating it as a legitimate function of the medical practitioner (like the amelioration of unbearable pain) and helping human beings to exercise complete control over their lives (which includes ending them voluntarily). Among Western nations, only the Netherlands makes this kind of activity legal, but after some years of experience, with induced deaths in the thousands, there are doubts about the advisability of continuing with the decriminalization of the practice. Some believe that all too frequently certain care-givers persuade the terminally ill to choose suicide and that in pain-laden circumstances the meaning of "free will" is distorted anyway, and manipulation becomes too easy.

Judaism and Christianity would classify this kind of activity as a form of euthanasia, to which they are strongly opposed, for they consider life a Divine gift that no one is permitted to throw away, except for some higher purpose (for instance, a mother sacrificing herself for her child) or as a means of escaping unspeakable suffering (like further existence in a concentration camp). There is little doubt, however, that the increase in longevity will also bring in its train renewed pressures to revisit this whole border territory between life and death. For the treatment of pain and depression do present serious problems, especially for older people.

Of late we have also heard much about the "quality of life" or the lack thereof. Someone existing for months in a comatose condition with little or no hope of recovery, or an Alzheimer's disease patient suffering from total oblivion while still facing years of "living"—these are the kinds of situations with which we are increasingly familiar. But Alzheimer patients may have an inner life of which we know nothing, while by external standards they do not enjoy a measurable "quality of life." Are we to do away with them, on the assumption that they do not want to exist in this condition but cannot express their wishes? Obviously that kind of decision making remains out of the question. The problem is that we usually look for solutions when often there are none, which is another way of saying that life is not always subject to "reasonable" rules, not even when one is old.

Getting Old—A Mixed Blessing.

Most people in human history have looked at getting old as a blessing. However, there have been notable exceptions. I will cite only a few.

Barzillai, a distinguished gentleman, lived around the year 1,000 BCE, and the Bible calls him "very old." He had done King David a great favor, and in gratitude the monarch invited him to move to Jerusalem and be his permanent guest. But Barzillai declined and gave this answer (which I have translated into colloquial English):

> I am now eighty years old and I no longer know what is up or down, how food or drink taste; and my hearing is so bad that I cannot hear when men or women sing-so why burden the lord my king with my presence?

Another biblical example (again translated colloquially): "Remember God when you are young and still possess your powers, before the bad days come when you will say: 'It is no longer any fun . . .'"

Shakespeare, a keen observer of his world if there ever was one, took this biblical description of old age a step further:

> Last scene of all,
> that ends this strange eventful history,
> is second childishness and mere oblivion,
> sans teeth, sans eyes, sans taste, sans every thing.

The most pessimistic summary was probably provided by Jean Paul Richter, a German writer who lived in the days of the French revolution: "What makes old age so sad is, not that our joys but that our hopes cease."

In the twentieth century, the redoubtable Simone de Beauvoir, a founder of existentialism, criticized writers for romanticizing old age and omitting its downside. She summarized her view by stating baldly that the last stage of life was "an insult." (Her book caused a flurry of scholarly investigations into inherited images of aging, with their biases and attendant socioeconomic structures and cultural processes.)

So how come most of us crave old age if it can hold such prospects? Maybe it is nothing more than our survival instinct, over which we have but limited control. Of course, there are those who decide they have had enough and life no longer justifies a continuing struggle with debility. Some attempt or commit suicide, others simply give up, knowingly or subconsciously, and with the will to live gone they may indeed die in short order.

May Sarton, poet and novelist of renown, set down the record of such struggles in her journal, which was published posthumously:

> I have begun this journal at a time of difficult transition because I am now entering real old age. At seventy-five I felt much more able than I do now. Forgetting where things are, forgetting names even of friends, names of flowers (I could not remember calendula the other day), what I had thought of writing here in the middle of the night—forgetting so much makes me feel disoriented sometimes and also slows me up. How to deal with continued frustration about small things like how to button my shorts, and big things like how to try for a few more poems. That is my problem.

In other places Sarton brims with life and future plans; and then again the journal entry tells us that occasionally her wish to die is staggering; and in a televised interview she told the audience how awful old age is. The publisher's blurb on the dust jacket sums up these sentiments: "Sarton continues to adjust to the feeling that she is a stranger in the land of old age."

She is not alone. In my drawer I found a clipping from some now unidentifiable newspaper, with a headline reading: "Nothing good about aging, old people say." I suspect that the samples quoted by the author came from a nursing home or some other institution, but I cannot be sure.

Question: "What are the best things about aging?"

Answers: "Best things? You think getting older has good things associated with it? You're crazy."

"Best things? Nothing!"

But there were other answers as well, and they confirm the obvious, that being old can range from good to bad, from struggle to contentment. No two oldsters experience their latter years in quite the same way.

"I haven't found that I'm aging."

"A good thing is still being around, and I know more things now, I've more experience."

The greatest fears recorded by the interviewer were: getting ill, being bedridden and a burden, being lonely, and losing memory—but almost half averred they had no fears. "I've lived a good life and there's no point being afraid of what's to come." Old people do think of death, but for many there is no dread connected with that thought.

Another journalist finds that, happily, there are also those who find aging a welcome experience:

"The reality is that growing old is one of God's most magnificent gifts . . . The great majority of older men and women are not in institutions, not senile, not poverty stricken, and above all are not willing to give up the passion of love which, if it is any good at all, gets better with age. Much better."

Similarly, cellist Pablo Casals wrote this at age 93:

Age is a relative matter. If you continue to work and absorb the beauty in the world about you, you find that age does not necessarily mean getting old. At least not in the ordinary sense. I feel many things more intensely than ever before, and for me life grows more fascinating . . . I do not think a single day passes by in my life in which I fail to look with fresh amazement at the miracle of nature. It is there on every side.

Gerontologists have identified certain psychological and social changes as people age. They gradually withdraw from activities (often because of physical deterioration), they become increasingly isolated (a consequence of the withdrawal and/or demise of family and friends), and by and by they disengage themselves from social or communal activities. These stages have become evident in my own tale of aging, as I have set forth above, in Chapter 1. In fact, writing this book has meant, for me, confronting both the downside of being old and the blessings that good old age can bring.

Subconsciously, we all know that either or both may be our lot, yet we take our chances and hope for the best. As for the negative view society takes of us, I have one strong conviction: If enough of us stand up for our dignity and our rights, we may yet manage to dent the attitude of rejection with which society confronts us and convince it that we still have a lot to offer. I am sure that if we not only say it but shout it with sufficient decibels, we may yet find willing ears.

Does Religion Help?

There is a general perception that people become more religious when they age. I presume that the impression is derived from three general sources:

1) that most persons in a congregation are likely to be grey-haired. (However, the preponderance of the old might signify nothing more than the absence of the young.)

2) that as one ages one thinks more frequently of dying and its spiritual consequences, if any, and therefore religious worship becomes more appealing as the years roll by. (This was certainly true yesterday, when the reality of heaven and hell was still part of most people's belief, and the growing nearness of death doubtlessly moved many to give added attention to their spiritual health. But, except for revival movements, the impact of theological perceptions has greatly weakened in North American society.)

3) religious faith helps people to live longer, and that is the reason one sees a lot of older folks in a religious setting. ("Can Religion Be Good Medicine?" asks an article in The Johns Hopkins Medical Letter. Among the reasons for a positive answer are these: attending services and prayer appear to diminish stress; religion seems to be a buffer against mental and

physical pain and help people to recover better from surgery. Last but not least, religious people are less likely to be depressed and commit suicide. God was pronounced dead a few decades ago, but that demise, too, has turned out to be an exaggeration.)

One might think that social scientists have given serious attention to this subject, but the opposite is true. In fact, one of the few studies of gerontology and religion claims that "gerontology has been colossally blind to the religious dimension of human aging."

A similar assessment is made by Martin E. Marty, who writes:

> The social scientists and others who study attitudes toward health and illness tend to overlook a major dimension that should be in their scope: the religious involvement of people.

General opinion has it that as one gets older and one's human convoy of family, friends, and associates shrinks, loneliness is all too often inevitable and darkens the light of day. But there is another side. The religious person, who feels the nearness of God, may escape loneliness and despair, especially if such belief is joined to the certainty of life after death.

Having spent the major part of my life in a religion-based environment, I have consistently found that people with a strong belief in a meaningful universe—which, after all, is the foundation of religion-have a sense that each person's life is important and that a loving God provides each one of us with the kind of life support that helps us to be at peace with the world. The above-quoted critiques have resulted in new investigations, some of them highly technical, and I have little doubt that a positive consensus will emerge, showing the salutary impact of faith and religious observance on the experience of aging. Also, a pattern of regular religious observance needs to be present, for it gives structure to one's life and becomes doubly meaningful when the structure provided by daily work has vanished from the life of the old. To be sure, physical problems may prevent them from attending public worship functions, but this is frequently replaced by personal spirituality. In her latter days, my mother became incapable of attending services, but she was never without her prayer book, which she read over and over again. When my wife and I would visit her on the Sabbath in her hospital room and turn it into a place of prayer, she would literally come to life and sing heartily and joyfully. I am convinced that her deep sense of religious integration was an important factor in her remarkably active aging and, finally, in her peaceful death.

African-Americans constitute the one group whose religious proclivities have been widely studied by social scientists, yet even here quantitative studies are rare when it comes to relating religion to aging. I have little doubt that meaningful results will be forthcoming in the near future and will support the impression that religious sentiment, belief and practice play an important positive role in the aging process.

The Internet: Reaching Beyond One's Grasp

This expression has never been meant to be taken literally, for it is a metaphor. It challenges us not to be satisfied with the ordinary but to do better by trying our best. The challenge will always be valid, but now the literal sense of the phrase suddenly makes sense as well.

Enter the Internet. No one who can afford a secondhand computer and a modest monthly connection fee need sit all alone, waiting for Godot. The world can be at one's fingertips: fabulous journeys to faraway places; chatting with strangers who might become friends; talking and listening, unfettered by time and distance. Here is one environment free of discrimination—though there will always be some who love to hate, even the old. As noted above, I have seen messages demonizing the aged as society's bloodsuckers and worse, but they represent an inconsequential verbal excrement of sick minds. Beyond this offal, however, are wondrous opportunities for meeting and talking, listening and learning, as well as pure and simple enjoyment.

In early 1999 my computer informed me that it could supply more than 10 million different items dealing with "seniors" or "aging" in the U.S. and nearly 2 million in Canada. I found that there were nearly 400 web sites focusing on centenarians, and that South Korea was a land with 1,151 people over 100 years old. I must admit being amused to learn that even when dealing with these long-lived survivors an author felt constrained to call them "the very elderly." Apparently she could not get herself to say that they were old.

Some suggestions for the wired who want to look around:

For U.S. government web sites, provided by the National Institute on Aging, the Administration on Aging, the Veteran Health Administration, and others, see www.seniorplace.com/government.asp

For statistical information: lib.lsu.edu/gov

For policy-related information on gerontology: www.smsu.edu/ger/gerlinks.html

The broadest access to health resources is provided by the (U.S.) National Library of Medicine's MEDLINE. Access is now free of charge: www.nlm.nih.gov/databases/freemedl.html

A comprehensive overview of Canadian oldsters, entitled *A Portrait of Seniors in Canada*, is found at statcan.ca/start.html

I also recommend subscribing to *Health After 50—The Johns Hopkins Medical Letter.* This newsletter, written by highly expert physicians, talks straightforwardly about simple as well as complex matters in a way that a lay person can easily grasp, and learn about what is or is not advised in certain circumstances, illnesses, and so forth. The latest discoveries are explained and new techniques endorsed or cautioned against. Thus, one issue contains articles on "Improved Eye Surgery To Sharpen Vision," the root cause of ringing in the ear, and a dozen other matters that will interest most of us. Of course, if you are lucky enough to have good longevity genes, you are likely to have a head start on the rest of your contemporaries.

In sum, there are endless opportunities for learning, asking, and answering as well as chatting. To be sure, punching a key does not substitute for meeting someone in the flesh, but one can be in touch with other people (and sometimes their emotions) without leaving home.

At this writing the International Year of Older Persons is already in full swing. When it runs out and welcomes the new millennium, the old will have gotten still older and more numerous. They will experience the pains and the joys of aging, its slower pace and its new-found vision. I hope that I will be around for a while to join them.

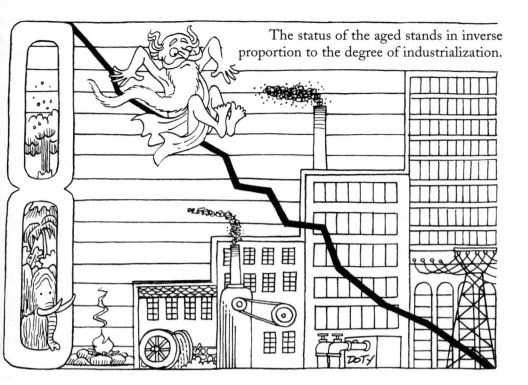

The status of the aged stands in inverse proportion to the degree of industrialization.

Then and Now, Here and There

Children Talk With Their Pens

How have the aged been treated in various times and cultures? I will let children lead off with their pencils and crayons. For sometimes the mouths of babes reveal reality without the censorship that social mores impose on adults. Some 14,000 children aged six to fourteen were asked to draw pictures of their grandparents. The results, covering thirty-three countries in many parts of the world, can be briefly summarized.

Despite their differences, there are striking similarities. Grandmothers are associated with the home (cooking, knitting, taking care of children); grandfathers are portrayed as being outside the home. Still, even here there are differences. Swiss children see grandpa as retired and passive, while Czech youngsters portray him smoking and drinking (which critics considered a form of activity).

Grandparents are portrayed either as living alone, rather than as part of society (so the drawings from most European industrialized societies), as having some role in the family, based on their above-noted gender (so, e.g., in Bulgaria), or as integrated with the parents as caregivers (in India).

Now to the way adults have treated or are treating their elders.

Simple Societies

I learned, first of all, that "the good old days" were not necessarily good. In my younger days the expression referred to the end of the nineteenth century, which is now a full hundred years in the past. Those were the days of the "gay nineties," and a bit of reading about that time will quickly tell you that those days were good and joyful only for a small percentage of the population, while for the rest there were sweat shops, poverty, discrimination of the worst sort, and other forms of inequality and want. But, looking through the nostalgic retrospector, it all looks good now—those good old days that the majority of us were fortunate to have escaped. Already more than 2,000 years ago the author of the biblical book of Koheleth (also known as Ecclesiastes, or the Preacher) wrote that anyone who thought that the past was better than the present, was a fool.

One should therefore not be surprised that a look at the olden days of human history by anthropologist Leo W. Simmons who made a thorough study of how the aged were treated in what he calls "primitive society," revealed a mixed bag of social goodies.

He studied seventy-one tribes around the world—for instance, Bushmen in South Africa, Haida in North America, Ainu in Japan—but surprisingly also lists pre-Columbian Aztecs and ancient Hebrews among the primitives. He offers no explanation for the Aztecs, whose society was complex and sophisticated. The Hebrews were included, he explains, because their records go back to antiquity. But if that was his motivation, why not take a look at the Sumerians, Babylonians, Greeks, or Romans? Aside from such quirks, however, Simmons has been the only one to study what I would call "simple societies" whose attitude toward the aging and old he investigated during the time of the Second World War. Here are some of his findings:

Food sharing. Especially in areas with severe climatic conditions, there was a tendency toward sharing what was available, and no one, young or aged, was excluded. But when the tribe came in contact with modernity, the sharing process declined.

Property Rights. Aged women appear to have had an edge in simple societies that depended for their livelihood on hunting and fishing, especially when matrilineal family organization prevailed, as it often did. Aged men had the advantage in farming and herding societies, where patriarchal structure was more prevalent, and especially so when the tribe came in contact with technically advanced societies.

Prestige. On the whole, aged members of the society were respected, in part because they had inherited status; but respect declined when the aged became disabled. Old men fared generally better than old women.

Use of the aged's knowledge. The old were usually respected for their knowledge of tradition, religion, and magic. They occupied a special rank when they acted as mediators between the tribe and supernatural powers.

The family. When forced from active participation in the life of the tribe, the old retreated to their immediate families, where during the latter days of their lives they found the greatest amount of security.

Approaching death. The social significance of dying was among the most varied features Simmons found. In some societies, the old might be honored if they decided to take their own lives or allowed themselves to be buried alive. In other tribes they might be abandoned, cast out, or killed by the closest of kin, while in still others they were carefully nurtured until their last breath. Thus, the hour of death might be feared or loved, despised or honored, reviled or considered an occasion for worship. An old warrior was especially honored when, dressed up in his best attire, he sought death in battle. In societies on the move in order to seek food, the aged were likely to be left behind—not unlike the practice of animal herds in search of a more suitable environment. Other researchers have noted that in some prehistoric societies old people who could no longer care for themselves would be turned out to the desert or jungle, where in short order they became nature's prey.

In historic times, the old fared fairly well in simple societies, which more often than not reserved a place of respect, even honor, for them. Death was accepted, not feared, and that acceptance might bring added reverence for the old who were facing it. But when such cultures developed more complex social structures, the aged were likely to become disadvantaged.

There is an additional difference worth mentioning. We in the West use chronology to describe old age, most other societies use functional descriptions. The latter look at the capacity of a person to contribute to society (like grandparenting or story telling), rather than go by rigid numbers or physical capacity to pigeonhole them.

The Jews

The basic religious text of Judaism is the Hebrew Bible, a collection of 36 sacred books that achieved its final form around the second century BCE in Palestine. Christianity arose in the same environment some 200 years later and called the Hebrew Bible the "Old Testament," since it added a new collection it called the "New Testament."

In later centuries, both Jews and Christians created their own additional literature that, together with the biblical books, forms the basis of their religious traditions. Since Western civilization is squarely built on the Bible and the traditions it evokes, and since reading it no longer constitutes the common literary experience of our time, I will devote extra space to it. The Bible is also the only fundamental scripture of any religion of which I know that devotes many passages to the subject of aging and the aged.

The most often quoted antique text on growing old comes from the biblical Book of Psalms. It describes the upper limits of our years and is not only a kind of popular statistics but also a commentary on aging:

> The years of our life are seventy,
> or, through special strength, eighty years,
> but the best of them are trouble and sorrow,
> and they fly away.

Clearly, reaching high numbers had (and still has) its downside and does not ensure a meaningful and serene existence-a pessimistic view, but then, life itself was tough. Then as now, not all the old were happy with their fate. The most telling negative experience of aging is contained in another verse in Psalms, where the poet cries out:

Do not cast me off in old age;
when my strength fails, do not forsake me!

Of course, many folk had better experiences, and in the popular view long life was generally considered a blessing from God. Dying like Abraham "at a good ripe age, old and contented" was seen as the ultimate reward for a life well lived.

The Bible contains also a collection of pithy sayings and loads of advice for young and old (ascribed to Koheleth). Its generally pessimistic view of life ends with a long poetic description of what happens to us in old age:

Remember your Creator in the days of your youth,
before the days of sorrow come and the years
of which you will say: "I have no pleasure in them";
before sun and light and moon and stars grow dark . . .

[Then follows a series of moving allegorical verses that enumerate the weakness and debility of old age, after which death enters.]

[Whereupon] the dust returns to the earth as it was,
and the breath of life to God who gave it.
Utter futility, said Koheleth,
all is futile.

But two oft-quoted proverbs have a kindlier perspective: "Grey hair is a crown of glory," one says, and another, "The glory of young men is their strength, and the beauty of old men is their grey hair."

The Torah and the rest of the Hebrew Bible contain also a series of admonitions about respect due to parents and other older people. But that did not guarantee that the aged were always treated right. The Bible admonishes people to get up for old people and respect them—which indicates that the reminder was necessary because not enough people considered oldsters worthy of respect. Even the famous phrase in the Ten Commandments that we should "honor father and mother" might not have been there if the number of offenders had not been substantial, and note that the call for parental honor and respect is repeated twice more! (In contrast, the Bible contains no commandment to love one's children.) We may assume that the Torah's warning not to curse and even not to strike our parents was issued because there had been enough occurrences to make such a law necessary (the penalty in both cases was death).

We read in a much later text (probably written at the end of the sixth century BCE) that a serious generation gap existed in Israelite society, for the prophet Malachi ends his book by predicting that when the day of human redemption comes, God will reconcile parents with their children and children with their parents. The generational conflict was evidently serious enough for the prophet to see its resolution as a paradigm for the ideal society. The old had problems in the olden days too.

The pessimistic view of Koheleth had a negligible impact on subsequent Jewish tradition. At the end of the second century CE, a code called the Mishnah was composed in Palestine by Rabbi Judah the Prince. Primarily devoted to a collection of Jewish religious law and tradition, it also contains general social and moral observations that go back many centuries. There we find a chronology of human life that lists the following sign posts:

> At the age of eighteen one is ready for marriage;
> at twenty for pursuing a vocation;
> at thirty one reaches the peak of vigor;
> at forty one understands [what life is all about];
> at fifty one can counsel others;
> at sixty one begins old age;
> at seventy one is grey-haired;
> at eighty one shows extra strength [to have lived that long)]
> at ninety one bends [beneath the weight of old age];
> at one hundred one is more dead than alive.

Unmistakably, a person who had reached the age of sixty was considered to have passed the peak of life and to have started the inevitable descent. The term "old age" here used was the Hebrew *ziknah*, derived from the word *zakein*, which designated an aged person.

This word is fascinating because it mirrors cultural history. It comes from a time when the aged were not relegated to retirement but often advanced to leadership, which is shown by the use of that term. For it also served to designate a leader, and the English "elder," in addition to denoting a church or tribal leader, is also the basis for "alderman."

A personal note on the biblical command to "rise before an aged person." Everyone I knew in my youth did this automatically, even as men used to do when a woman of any age entered the room. Older persons were literally assured a seat in a public conveyance, for someone would at once get up for them. One of the differences I noted when I first settled in the United States was the growing disregard of this biblical demand. I am pleased when someone yields a seat to me—not only because it is more comfortable to sit than to stand, but also because I delight to see that some youngsters are brought up with respect for the old. (When it does happen, it usually turns out that the polite youth is a recent immigrant, which becomes evident when I express my thanks.)

In the millennia since the Bible was composed, the Jews have lived primarily in Diaspora, where they generally had their own communities, organized to create an environment that reflected biblical commands. It became a rule to treat elders with respect, and when they could not fend for themselves or live with their families, they were afforded housing in dignified homes for the aged. In my Jewish communal experience, I have found that while raising funds is often hard, it becomes relatively easy when it is for the purpose of caring for the old.

The Christians

Keep in mind that Christianity incorporated the Hebrew Bible into its own tradition and called it the "Old Testament." The first Christians were Jews, and the Jewish view of aging became part of the Church and its teaching, though the new religion's membership soon became overwhelmingly Gentile. Additional comments in the Gospels are the following:

Luke opens with stories of elders like Zechariah, Elizabeth, Anna, and Simeon, whose contribution is thus strongly underlined. Paul enjoined Timothy to extend "double honor" to older men and widows and warned against judging oldsters hastily and prejudicially.

Of special interest is the intimation of a generation gap that mirrored the above-noted social condition depicted by the prophet Malachi a half millennium earlier. Says Paul, "You fathers must not goad your children to resentment, but give them the instruction and correction which belong to a Christian upbringing."

Later, two Renaissance authors, Luigi Cornaro (1475–1566) and Gabriele Paleotti (1522–1597) had a significant influence on later Church attitudes toward the aging. The former, a Venetian nobleman, stressed moderation and self-discipline as the best roads to longevity. He lived to the age of 91 and observed, "I think my present age, although it is very advanced, is the pleasantest and finest of my life. I would not exchange my age and my life for the most flourishing youthfulness."

Paleotti was a cardinal who wrote a book entitled *De bono senectutis (On the Good of Old Age)*.

> [He] was one of the great Christian humanists of the Renaissance, and a disciple of Cicero in his philosophy of age, transforming the Stoic Nature into the Christian God. Paleotti held that the sadness of old age could to some extent be relieved by forms of relaxation like music, games, baths and pleasure tours. But these left the inner cause of sadness still intact, and it consisted of the awareness of diminishing time and approaching death, and the collapse of self-regard occasioned by the assault of the public's stereotypes of the aged as miserly, timid, suspicious, and disagreeable.

I find the cardinal's last observation a remarkable comment on a situation that has not visibly changed in the 400 years since. In 1976, the Catholic Bishops of the United States issued a statement entitled "Society and the Aged: A Reconciliation," which constitutes a strong critique of the pervasive rejection of the aged. One of its wide range of considerations is expressed as follows:

> Society's negative image of the elderly reinforces their own negative self-image. The result of this unfortunate process is a tragically wasted human resource. The elderly are denied their God-given right to develop their potential to the fullest at every stage of life; at the same time, society is denied the fruits of that development.

Pope John Paul II has repeatedly emphasized the need to see older people as part of a continuum rather than as a separate group. Addressing seniors at a rally in Canada, he said:

> The value of life lies in who you are, not in what you possess or are able to do. Your life shows the continuity of the generations and gives you a horizon from which to judge new events and discoveries. You remind the world of the wisdom of earlier generations, while you contribute your insights to this one. . . . Old age is the crowning point of earthly life, a time to gather in the harvest you have sown. It is a time to give of yourselves as you have never done before.

Islam

The fundamental idea that underlies Islam's respect for the aged is intimately related to the concept of God as the source of all life and is reflected in the Quranic statement:

> It is Allah Who
> Created you in a state
> Of weakness, then
> Gave (you) strength after weakness,
> Then, after strength, gave (you)
> Weakness and grey hairs:
> He creates what He will;
> He is the Wise, the Powerful.

A person's humanity is not affected by age; all people, of whatever age are to be respected as God's children. The family is the central place where respect for others find their validation, and it is the parents who above all are entitled to respect in their old age, regardless of any weakness or disability from which they might suffer.

Parents thus are a paradigm for the old and infirm, who should be treated with the same kindness and respect that one would extend to one's own parents. (Further on Muslim practice, see below, the discussion of Tunisia.)

The Greeks and Romans

The Greek term for "old age" was *geras,* which gave its name to the gerousia, a Spartan body of elders who had to be more than 60 years of age. (The words "gerontology" and "geriatrics" are derived from *geras.*) When we scan the literature of Greek civilization produced in the first millennium BCE we see a rather negative picture. Thus, Sophocles has the aged chorus singing in *Antigone:*

> Of happiness the summit and crowning part
> Is wisdom, and to hold the gods in reverence.
> This is the law: that, beholding the stricken
> Heart of pride brought down, we learn only when
> We are old.

But the poet had also a softer word to say when he spoke of old age as teaching all things, in addition to bringing the ravages of time. He had good reason to do so, for he himself lived into his nineties and experienced both the continued acclaim of his contemporaries and the rapacious desires of his son, who tried to have him declared incompetent and thereby get hold of his estate. But when the jury examined the poet's mental acumen, he read to them portions of his latest work, *Oedipus at Colonus,* and was not only declared fit to conduct his affairs but was accorded public acclaim in the court room.

Euripides has old Hecuba (whose legs could no longer support her) exclaim:

> O helplessness of age!
> Too old, too weak to stand.

Another author of the Greek classical period, Mimnermus, ruminated that he did not wish to live past 60 (then considered old), for he did not want to have to deal with poverty and illness. Plato, on the other hand, has old Cephalus opine that it is not age itself but people who determine its effects:

The man who has a calm and happy disposition will scarcely feel the pressure of age. The man who is of the opposite disposition finds that both youth and old age are equally troublesome.

Similarly Aristophanes, whose old characters complain that what they did in years past is forgotten, that the public no longer cares for them when they get old, and that they are jeered at in the streets and persecuted by the young.

In sum, the picture drawn from Greek literature is painted mostly in dark colors, primarily because poverty appears to have been a major social consequence of aging. (We know that this has been history's experience in most lands and ages; not until the twentieth century did the old receive some relief in this respect. But even now, poverty, particularly among old women, remains a vexing problem.)

Greek culture became the underpinning of Roman civilization, which added to the understanding of the aged through the writing of one of its most famous men. The first book on old age was composed in ancient Rome by Marcus Tullius Cicero, politician, rhetorician par excellence, philosopher and poet. Called *De senectute (On Old Age)*, it extolled the advantages and serenity that long life could bring. I have rehearsed his arguments in detail in chapter 3, above.

North American Natives

In earlier days, the traditions of our aboriginal population were transmitted orally, with the old functioning as guardians of a precious heritage and being honored as such. This aura of respect for the elders is reflected in many tribal customs. Thus, families that honor their elder members gain in respect. Their children turn to them to learn ceremonial behavior, and public veneration of them underscores the Native cultures' conscious divergence from the surrounding population and its modern habits. In the Dene community of Alaska and western Canada, young boys and girls are expected to help their elders, bringing them wood, hauling water for them, and being as helpful as possible. They are being taught that long life will lie ahead for them if they care for their elders.

The Cree of west-central Canada and the United States call Fire, Water, Wind, and Water (nature's elemental powers) "Grandfathers," whose task it is to help the Great Spirit. They have been here since the world was created, and of course their very name betokens great respect.

The repetition of the grandparent example is not accidental. Native cultures are less caught up with chronological rigidity than the non-Native culture surrounding them; theirs is a functional society, where aging members are respected for their role in fostering continuity. Grandparents usually perform ceremonial rites in front of children, so that by watching them, "children are taught appropriate ceremonial behavior toward their elders."

Asian Perspectives

Since this book primarily reflects our Western society, the following is but a bird's eye view of the continent where more than half of humanity dwells, briefly highlighting various religious perspectives on aging.

Buddhism: The basic thought was laid down in the Buddha's direction for behavior in a religious order. The rule for monks was to be ranked by seniority and not by previous standing in society. This rule was expanded to embrace all society, which reserved a special place for its most senior members. Burma is one nation where to this day Buddhism, in its various sects, forms the majority culture.

Among the Burmese who are not yet exposed to the ways of the West, the conversation between people who are just introduced starts with the question: "How old are you?" A faux pas, according to the Westerners, but actually a polite gesture showing the willingness to treat the other party with due respect. . . . It is seniority, always seniority, that decides how a well-bred person addresses and speaks to another person.

Common practices in school or public observances during the Fall are designed to honor older persons (teachers among them!), and these, in return, must make sure that they deserve such accolades. The Western term "generation gap" is unfamiliar in this part of the world.

Confucianism and Taoism: These two form the cultural/religious backdrop of Chinese civilization. Confucius lived and taught in China at the same time as the Second Isaiah preached to his Israelite compatriots in Babylonian exile (sixth century BCE). The center of his teaching was *jen*, that is, "to love others joyously and from one's innermost heart." Loving parents became a core prescription, and therewith the old assumed an ever-increasing role in the life of China, which in time embraced Confucian philosophy as its primary thought system. *The Classic of Filial Piety* (one of the 13 basic texts) had an enormous influence in establishing respect for the elderly as a fundamental rule for society and remained operative in China for two millennia, down to our day. Thus, old age was not only no hindrance for occupying public office, it was a powerful recommendation.

Another of the classics of Confucianism is the *Book of History*, which lists five "blessings of life": long life, riches, health of body and mind, love of virtue, and natural and timely death.

Confucianists believe that one can enjoy happiness chiefly through the gift of long life. Later Confucianists say that long life enables people to enjoy life fully, gives knowledge as well as the ability to make what has been impossible possible, and advances understanding and learning. . . . The Five Blessings are obtained only if one is obedient to the will of the Supreme.

The importance of human health is therefore a mirror of the Confucian outlook on life. But not only one's own health needs to be safeguarded; others' well-being too belongs to the sphere of human responsibility.

Ekiken Kaibara dedicated several pages in his *Yojokun* (*The Motto for Health*) to the care of the old. Young people, he said, should make it possible for the old to enjoy life and satisfy their needs as much as possible, but, he added, when younger folk fail in their duty, the oldsters should understand that such failing is "the way of the world." Ekiken was apparently a forerunner of modern diet watchers, for he advised the aged not to overeat.

Despite political upheavals, Chinese culture has largely preserved the traditions that accord the aged a special place of honor, at times even approaching a form of worship. A classic work, the *Li Chi (Book of Ritual)* details the care that is due the old. For instance, it punishes patricide more severely than other murders: The offender will suffer a lingering death, and even the schoolmaster who instructed him is to be executed (what an encouragement to become a teacher!), and as a final indication of esteem for the departed, the bones of the killer's own grandparents are to be exhumed and scattered. Aside from such extreme examples another fact is more convincing: Until recently, the Chinese government consisted almost exclusively of old men who elsewhere would have been retired years before.

I cannot close this brief sketch of Confucianism without drawing attention to a saying ascribed to the Master, for it should be read in comparison as well as contrast to the text of the Mishnah that I cited above:

> At 15 I set my heart on learning;
> at 30 I was firmly established;
> at 40 I had no more doubts;
> at 50 I knew the will of heaven;
> at 60 I was willing to listen to it;
> at 70 I could follow my heart's desire
> without transgressing what was right.

Tao is the term for "The Way" that people should follow in order to live in harmony with natural law. (The word parallels the Hebrew *halachah*, which also means "the way" that Jews should follow to obey God's will.) Like Confucianism, Taoism combines philosophy and practical guidance for living, but while the former stresses duty, learning, and ethics, the latter addresses itself primarily to the mental and physical health of the individual, though its rites do have a religious tone. It teaches that by following its prescriptions perfectly we can avoid death and attain a kind of "celestial immortality." Sin shortens life, good deeds prolong it. Longevity is therefore a sign of good living, and those who attain it deserve the respect of the people.

Taoist thought has permeated Chinese culture and served as a link between Confucian tradition and ancient folk ways. It joyously affirms life and therefore opposes the negative view of earthly existence that characterizes Buddhism. Korea, Vietnam, and Japan have been heavily influenced by Taoism.

India: The subcontinent is basically a two-religion country, with Buddhism and Hinduism covering most of its huge population. The latter represents a conglomeration of religious traditions that have generally lived in harmony with one another. However, there have been violent confrontations on occasion, even fairly recently. (Religious tensions exist also between the majority religions and both Sikhism and Islam, but these confrontations have their origin primarily in territorial rather than religious aspirations.)

Buddhism and Hinduism arose out of an old agrarian civilization, in which different age groups lived together. A complex kinship system provided everyone a particular place at every stage of life, and allotted the aged a relatively secure position. But what was easy in the village or small town has become more difficult in the metropolitan areas, though extended family life manages to survive to some degree. Western influence, however, with its emphasis on technology and material progress, has weakened matriarchal and patriarchal traditions. and thereby has been less than beneficial to the aged, especially in the large cities, Still, India also remains the land where the tradition of renunciation was born, a teaching that is seen as the final human liberation and as giving those who embrace it a special place of moral power, regardless of their age. It was an important element in the spiritual force exerted by Mahatma Gandhi.

From the lives of Gandhi and Swami Tamananda we can see the importance of the religious dimension in securing a place for the elderly in society, and in providing meaning and purpose to their lives. In turn, the respect and admiration accorded them by those about them attest to the fact that they serve the needs of their fellow men in helping to bring them into touch with the sacred dimension. And in the process they help others to face with courage and purpose threats that would otherwise be unnerving and disorienting.

All of this, while understandable in India, may seem strange to Westerners, who are on the whole so secularized that mystery and religion appear as marginal oddities rather than central concerns. Yet when it comes to death and dying, religion reassumes its place of importance in the West as well, supporting Mircea Eliade's broad observation that "religion is the paradigmatic solution for every existential crisis."

Japan: Traces of this nation's paternalistic past are still in evidence, and ancestor-based Shinto has remained the quasi-state religion. This has tended to protect the integrated position of elders, and high age has continued to be a source of prestige. The country has a national "Respect for the Aged Day." There is a relative scarcity of nursing and retirement homes, because it is the cultural assumption that adult children will care for their parents at home. Public transportation reserves "silver" seats for the elderly or infirm. (We have them in Toronto, too. While people of all ages occupy them, they are likely to vacate the space when requested.)

Another perception contributes to the respectful attitude that Japanese generally reserve for the old: People are not acknowledged to have mastered any art or business until they have reached the middle years, and meaningful promotion does not take place until then. The North American veneration of youth is conspicuously absent. "The religious image of *okina*, the symbol of an old person's wisdom and mental and spiritual maturity, lies deeply embedded in Japanese consciousness."

But the chords of tradition have discordant notes as well. Sei Shonogan (about 1000 CE) views the elderly—that is, those past 40—as ugly and aggravating, and some 200 years later the monk Kenko suggests that oldsters past 40 should gracefully die or, if they do not, should live somewhere secluded from public view and contact. To be sure, he has also a few good words about certain older men, but not about women, whose value is their youth and beauty. With both gone, what point is there to their hanging around? Of that genre is also a legend about the Obasute Mountains where the old were left to die.

I end these often contradictory sentiments with this encouraging metaphor: "The flower that is youth implies the withered flower that is old age, yet the dried blossom is no less a flower because it is withered. Aging is life itself."

Africa

This continent contains a vast multitude of national, tribal, and religious traditions whose diversity cannot be adequately dealt with in this book. In general terms, it may be said that where familial relationships remain strong, extended family responsibility protects the aged. For instance, in Nigeria (the most populous nation on the continent):

There is no facility for institutionalized care for the elderly, except as a long-term hospital patient. There are no provisions for non-clinical residential accommodation (such as geriatric or old people's homes, nursing homes, homes for the aged or dependent).

The Nigerian novelist, Chinua Achebe, wrote *Things Fall Apart*, in which he respectfully traces the trials of Okonkwo, an aging leader who attempts to stem the cultural decline of a society whose ancient values he cherishes.

In Tunisia, an Arab nation that is overwhelmingly Muslim, taking someone to a nursing home appears shocking to most people, a sign of decadence and abandonment, particularly when the subject (especially an aged male parent) is made aware of the fact that he is "useless." Similarly condemned is the occasional practice of casting aside elderly women when they can no longer perform normal household tasks, especially the care of grandchildren while parents are at work. This critique reflects the Muslim demand to accord the aged proper respect.

Other Voices

In Central and South America, even within some nations, attitudes about the aged differ sufficiently so that generalizations are not helpful. While the population is overwhelmingly Roman Catholic, it also features a measure of native religious traditions. Thus, among the Nambicuara of Mato Grosso in Brazil, the same word is used for both "old" and "ugly," which cannot, however, be taken to reflect a general view of the aged in the country.

North American habits and views—both positive and negative—have had an increasing influence on the culture of the Americas. Costa Rica is distinguished in that it has no army and has used the funds thus saved for education and social services. It has managed to blend local traditions with Western concepts, and the elderly seem therefore to be comparatively well situated, especially since the economic condition of the nation has been fairly good and poverty rather contained.

Australia and New Zealand are thoroughly Western in language and tradition, but Australia's aboriginal population has its own view of life and therefore of old age. Thus, the Kowrarega tribe's word for "old man" is *ke–turkeka*, which actually means something akin to "superman"—a startling opposite to the above-noted synonyms in a Brazilian tribe. When I visited New Zealand some years ago, I found the Maori minority to cherish certain customs resembling those of the Jews, including visible respect for their elders.

Summary

So, what can one say about the treatment of the aged around the world today? While it is risky to generalize, the so-called "modernization theory" dares to suggest that the more modern a society has become the less the old are valued, and that in fact the status of the aged stands in inverse proportion to the degree of industrialization. Added thereto is the factor of social and religious change: The more traditional and stable the community, the more the old are valued; the greater the change, the lower their status and their impact.

That leaves limited room for the old, unless of course they band together and try to do something about it.

The closing years of life resemble
the end of a masquerade party,
when the masks are removed.
Attributed to Arthur Schopenhauer

Let me not pray to be sheltered
from dangers, but to be fearless in
facing them.
Rabindranath Tagore

Everything living has
a deadline.

POSTLUDE

Looking Ahead

The Shrinking Convoy

We go through life accompanied by human convoys of varying sizes. When we are small, our parents and siblings are our chief convoy; thereafter, it is our peers; at the peak of mid-life, the people in our workplace and social circle form our environment; and when we retire the convoy begins to shrink. Contemporaries die and we are left behind with our ever diminishing convoy, wondering about our future.

A view toward the future underlies the conscious and subconscious of every living creature. Childhood, youth, and young adulthood have expansive visions of what life will bring; middle age begins to set limits, and old age experiences them, yet bringing new posssibilities in its train.

Mother started to live when she was 71 and became a full-time volunteer. Old age turned out to be the crown of her life, and when she died after nearly 103 years she had become a famous woman. If I have her genes for longevity, I may have an opportunity to emulate her to some degree-and then again, I may not. I think of my father when it comes to philosophy; I think of Mother when I look ahead. And, having observed her at very close range for over 30 years (she lived a couple of blocks away and we saw each other regularly), I could follow her way from unbounded energy to giving up in the end. It is not surprising, therefore, that with every passing year I ruminate more often on my own decline. Though my ultimate future is certain, the how and when leave ample room for optimism.

Fortunately, my mental capacities have remained unaffected, and writing as well as lecturing is giving me continuing satisfaction. But I know that here, too, a slow downhill journey will commence some day, and it is good that I am not advised when that will be. The constant reminder of potential fragility is my increasing difficulty with name retrieval—which is occasionally quite bothersome and is not diminished by the fact that scientists are not quite sure why this is often the first sign of mental aging. People used to believe that this the beginning of progressive forgetfulness and heralded a general decline of mental capacity, something that gerontologists have squarely refuted.

To be sure, no older person's body is likely to be anywhere near the strength of its younger years, but that same conclusion is not warranted for the brain. Its rate of deterioration is usually minimal in reasonably healthy aging people, a finding that, happily, my own self-observation is able to endorse. How long that will last I do not know; but I am grateful that for the time being my grey cells still welcome a diet of new knowledge and store the old in accessible fashion.

The major reduction I suffer lies elsewhere. Each year my personal environment suffers a diminution in the number of friends and acquaintances, who have moved into the beyond. My convoy—so large in my middle years—is shrinking visibly. Scanning the obituaries in the daily newspaper has become a must. When and what will they read about me? I wonder occasionally.

The Unmentionable

Death and what precedes it is a difficult conversation topic, and I rarely find someone who is willing to talk to me about it. Maybe people fear that such conversations attract evil spirits who are just waiting for us to trip the fatal wires through imprudent speech and thereby set off the implosion of self-destruction. Or this avoidance of the subject may have to do with something else altogether, says Elisabeth Kübler-Ross, who dragged the subject of death out of the closet:

> The more we make advancements in science, the more we seem to fear and deny the reality of death. How is this possible?
>
> We use euphemisms, we make the dead up as if they were asleep, we ship the children off to protect them from the anxiety and turmoil around the house if the patient is fortunate enough to die at home, we don't allow children to visit their dying parents in the hospitals, we have long and controversial discussions on whether patients ought to be told the truth . . .
>
> I think there are many reasons for this flight away from facing death calmly. One of the most important facts is that is that dying nowadays is more gruesome in many ways, namely, more lonely, mechanical, and dehumanized; at times it is even difficult to determine technically when the time of death has occurred.

Though the famous doctor managed to puncture the veil of secrecy surrounding human demise, most people still refuse to face this "ultimate scandal," as it is occasionally called. I sat through long sessions with families (including my own), trying to persuade them that the dying need communication and honesty, not denial and deception. Why deny them the opportunity to share last words with their loved ones? And why deny it to the survivors? On the rare occasions when such good-byes did occur, both the dying and the survivors experienced a sense of peace, and the closure became a sacred moment. A widow(er) will always remember the dying spouse's encouragement to carry on with life and the confession of love that prompted it, while the children report the meaningfulness of the blessing they received from their parent. But all too often the dying or their families or both fear what they think will be a confrontation with their own fears and cannot manage to obtain the peace they crave.

Strange: When doctor or nurse pay the terminally ill a brief visit they will often say, "You're doing okay" or something to that effect. The patient knows it is not true, and the caregiver knows that the patient knows.

But who has the time and energy to enter into a discussion about life and death and the myriad questions that might arise? Lately, medical schools have been teaching their students how to meet these moments more constructively, but it is tough to be honest when one cannot be sure that it is really desired. For in our climate of continuing death denial, a lot of people, though aware that deception surrounds them, may not want to be confronted with the truth—at least that is the message I often heard from the family. She or he will lose hope, I would be told, and meanwhile the patient is left with anything but personal dignity. I found that most frequently it was the family and not the patient who did not want to air the unmentionable subject. Without exception, however, spouse and children who do have the chance to talk openly to the dying will report the moments of parting as an experience they will always remember and cherish. I hope when my time comes I will manage to do what our forefather Jacob did: assemble the family and bless them one by one. Too bad that the blessing of dear ones is an elixir not carried in pharmacies or health stores. It is carried only in the storehouse of love, understanding, and courage to face the inevitable. When we do this we also enrich the days left to us. Professor Morris Swartz of Brandeis University, stricken with Lou Gehrig's disease, said in his final days that only as we learn how to die do we learn how to live.

Writing a Living Will

My experience as a counselor teaches me that people are likely to be receptive to talking about life's end when not death but debilitating illness is the subject matter. They usually know families with someone incapable of making personal decisions, especially when it comes to attaching or withdrawing life support systems. I have found that children or spouses of the terminally ill are beset with anxiety and guilt when permitting nature rather than machines to take over and let their dear one die. No rabbi, priest, pastor, or imam can empty the basket of regrets and doubts that is left behind. "Did you ever discuss this whole issue with the deceased?" I would ask, and the answer was rarely positive. From this, my wife and I have drawn one simple conclusion for ourselves: We will not let each other or our children bear this particular burden and will make the decision for them and the doctors.

Each of us has drawn up two documents that state our desires in certain directions, just in case we should become unable to express them because of incapacity. One deals with matters contained in a "general power of attorney" and the other with personal care. In doing so we had legal advice, which is necessary to make sure that the provisions of provincial or state law (where they exist) are complied with.

The document dealing with personal care might contain thoughts such as these:

> I hereby expressly declare my intended wish that I be cared for in my own home to the greatest extent possible and for the longest period possible, rather than being cared for in a chronic care institution of any kind, including a nursing home or an institution dedicated to the care of the elderly. In this regard, I wish appropriate nursing and health care also be provided for me in my home, to the greatest extent possible.
>
> I do not wish to have my life unduly prolonged by any course of treatment or other medical procedure that offers no reasonable expectation of my recovery from life-threatening physical or mental incapacity, except as any such course of treatment or medical procedure may be necessary for the relief of suffering. I desire my personal attorney for personal care, _____, to follow my written and oral directions which I may give or prepare before or after the date of execution of this power of attorney for personal care. [There might follow a clause indemnifying that person against any claims that might arise in connection with his or her making such relevant decisions on behalf of the patient.]

These desires reflect the fact that my wife and I still have each other and have a home (actually, an apartment). What the written text expresses are hopes and desires; they will help the capacitated make informed decisions that will not engender the burden of guilt. It is as uncomplicated as that.

The Hope of Immortality

As long as humans have inhabited the earth, they have wondered about death: Is it the moment that betokens the end of an individual in the same way it seems to do for animals? We kill them and eat their carcasses and are not worried about their souls, if any. Are we then different in that there is something of us humans that lives on?

One cannot really answer that question without determining what sets us apart from the rest of creation. Is it a "soul" or "spirit" that is not found elsewhere? This is a tough question, because we do not know how animals think and whether they have a sense of self in the same, or at least a similar, way humans do. For nowadays we acknowledge that certain animals do make decisions consciously; the old idea that dogs, apes, dolphins, and a host of others act on instinct only has long been abandoned. How far down in the scale of evolution this goes is unknown at present.

What, then, sets us apart? Clearly, we have something they do not have. Brain size? Elephants and whales have bigger brains. A sense of self? Possibly, but we do not know. The Bible does not dwell on this subject; it merely states in its opening chapter that God made us the apex of creation and gave us rulership over other earthly creatures. The book does have a word for spirit, *nefesh*, but that same word also describes animals and humans. No help there. The fact is that the existence of a soul cannot be proven and is therefore part of our belief system. Most of us are convinced that there is more to being human than having a brain, however magnificently it is structured. It is that special extra that, to speak in biblical terms, made us human and that caused God to set us apart as creatures with whom the Divine could have a personal relationship. Hence, those who believe in some form of immortality also believe in the existence of a spiritual add-on we call soul, and those who do not are likely to deny the separate existence of souls as well.

With some notable exceptions (of which more below), people throughout the ages of recorded history have generally believed that we have souls and that there is some form of immortality. Their religions taught them that this hope was founded in revelation, reason, tradition, or some other trustworthy source. Of course, no one has ever died and returned to report what happened. A cautionary rabbinic tale that warns against too much metaphysical speculation tells of four wise men who did have a chance to look at "the other side"—"Paradise," or the world beyond. Only one returned unscathed, and he decided to keep to himself whatever knowledge he had garnered. The story thus has a bottom line: Do not ask questions about it; the exercise might be harmful to you, and in any case you will not get an answer. Of course, this has not kept people from asking.

So, what do they hear in return? Everything from "I don't know because I can't know" to the most detailed descriptions of Heaven, Hell, and everything between, from Dante and Milton to the latest TV preacher. Various belief systems have raised such speculations to the status of dogmas. Among these are ideas of incarnation (higher beings taking on human form), reincarnation (human souls made flesh again), transmigration of souls, bodily resurrection, and immortality of one's soul. The kings of ancient Egypt were believed to be incarnations of the god Ra; after they suffered ordinary death they were preserved in special chambers (found in pyramids) and outfitted with every item thought necessary for their journey into the next life. Traditional Jews believe that the dead will be resurrected when the Messiah comes, and that meanwhile, the righteous enjoy a blissful existence in the world beyond; Christians hold that Jesus assumed (or returned to) divine stature; and Buddhists consider their religious founder to have been an incarnation of the god Vishnu—paralleling the belief of Hindus regarding Rama.

Where does that leave ordinary people who do not aspire to such exalted distinction? If they are products of a religious environment they are likely to cherish some thought of immortality, not of the body, which they know decomposes, but of the soul—whatever that may mean. If they do hold such hopes for themselves and for their dear ones, they are in fact modern-day followers of Plato's teachings, namely, that body and soul dwell together temporarily but are essentially distinct from each other. The former disappears, the latter lives on in some way. The Greek sage wrote a fascinating treatise on the subject, called *Phaedon*, where he puts his words in the mouth of Socrates, who argues that the logic of life demands that the human spirit survive the bodily shell.

Many others, however, brand such ideas as mere figments of human hope and claim to boot that such inventions cleverly manipulate the poor and dispossessed of the earth. For these unfortunates are thereby led to believe that their present misery is but a temporary prelude to the real thing, to Paradise, where they will be amply recompensed for what they missed here below. So be patient, they are told, the real goodies are yours in days to come, but meanwhile you have to be satisfied, and may be punished with hellfire if you do not shape up. This faith structure, so its critics claim, became a tool of church bodies and state powers to keep the human sheep docile, and thus such theology served political rather than spiritual ends.

On the other hand, the denial of divine reward and punishment is no more provable than its reality. If leading a decent and upright life promises believers a suitable recompense, it has produced some of the most generous and selfless people, without whom society would be much the poorer. This does not prove or disprove anything, but indubitably this belief responds to the deepest needs of humanity.

Scores of good books and treatises have argued for some form of immortality. The most convincing "proof" I have so far encountered arises from one of the best known laws of physics, the Law of Conservation of Matter and Energy. It holds that matter may change its form but never disappears. Thus, when a piece of wood is burned, the wood changes into heat and ashes. These are likely to change further, but the components will remain as matter or energy in some form. Now, if matter is, so to speak, immortal, is it logical to believe that the spirit is not, when in fact it appears as the dominant part of existence as we know it?

I do not put this rumination forward in order to "prove" immortality; I do, however, find it a reasonable belief. Still, belief it remains, and it happens to be mine too. Something of me, as of everyone, becomes (to continue the analogy with matter) either ashes or heat, some of it forgotten and part of the ash heap of existence like my body, and part of it (I hope) worthy to be joined to the all-encompassing spirit of God.

Will it be a conscious personal existence as it is now? Will I once again meet my late brother, my parents, and my departed friends? I for one do not believe that—but if I am wrong, so much the better. I do believe that the best of me will indeed be immortal. How much and in what fashion I do not and cannot know. Becoming part of all the others who have striven for ideals and, being human, have fallen short of achieving them fully is a fate piously to be wished for. In sum, I find immortality a good possibility, but I do not consciously strive to earn it. The standards I have tried to follow are, I hope, not unpleasing to God and my failures not too grievous, and that is as far as I can go. No one put this better than Mark Twain: "Let us endeavor so to live that when we die even the undertaker will be sorry." Amen.

And what about earthly immortality, which is more accessible to comprehension? Yes, children and grandchildren will remember me, but after they are gone my name will strike no audible chords. The books I have written are mostly forgotten already; some will survive for a while and then join the others on library shelves, where they will gather dust either as paper creations or CD-ROMs.

We have a family burial plot in Toronto. We have lived here for nearly forty years, and it has become our home. Mother was buried here, but Dad, who died fifty years ago, was interred in St. Paul, Minnesota, where we resided at the time. For years I wondered whether or not to move his remains to Toronto, but I decided to let him rest where he is. The stone that identifies him stands at the entrance of the cemetery, and by being there he silently testifies to our one-time residence in that capital city where we raised our children. It is a dead man's testimony, for he himself did not live to enjoy St. Paul, where he might have had the best years of his life.

Whenever I think of him, I am grateful that he opened for me the gates of history and urged me to read as many books as possible in the splendid library we had at home. The older I become the more I miss him. Perhaps that is the reason why I seem to tell so many tales about him and quote the sayings he imparted to me. The puzzle that stands at the head of the Preface to this book is but one example. Alas, no one will be left to talk about him when I am gone.

What If?

What will happen if new medical advances will make us (or rather, those who follow us) live longer and longer, tending ever more toward earthly immortality? No doubt the attempt will be made and will raise lots of hope, but also lots of fear. We already have trouble providing sustenance for all human beings, so that a serious and ever growing increase in our numbers will likely strain our resources badly. And even if new technology solves this problem too, there remains a fundamental question about the way human life will unfold. It has always been assumed that the underlying urge that drives us to make our lives meaningful and satisfying is fueled by the knowledge that we have a limited time to accomplish these goals. But if that urge dries up because we can wait till tomorrow and tomorrow, what will that do to human creativity? Will it fundamentally change our character? Why worry about anything if I can do it ten years from now or later? What kind of people would a "*mañana* society" produce? Maybe we should reread *Gulliver's Travels* and get reacquainted with the Struldbrugs, people who live forever:

> They were not only opinionative, peevish, covetous, morose, vain, talkative; but incapable of friendship, and dead to all natural affection. . . .
>
> The reader will easily believe, that from what I have heard and seen, my keen appetite for perpetuity of life was much abated.

A final word on the ever-expanding world of technology. It is at heart neutral and can be turned toward evil and toward good. A Conference on Aging and Technology that was held in Jerusalem a few years ago held out many hopes for improved methods of communication. Accessible to everyone, young or old, they will keep the aged more integrated in society than they are at this stage of human history. Thus, for instance, television has traditionally been one-directional: The machine presents a program, and the viewer looks and listens. Tomorrow's TVs will be participatory, whereby the viewer will have a chance to enter into conversation with the program. The technique is already in use on personal computers, where "chat rooms" have become increasingly popular. Something of this kind is now being adapted for television, which will improve life for the lonely, many of whom are old. I hope that this will indeed be one of the wonders of the new millennium's scientific endeavors.

As long as we are capable of learning and growing we will be privileged to eat the fruits garnered from the Tree of Time. I would urge the reader to keep in mind the pleading of Lynn Adler who has made the "old old" her special focus:

> There is a positive side to aging, and there are many people of advanced age who are interested in remaining a part of the world

around them and who want to remain active and engaged in life to the greatest extent possible. Centenarians help dispel this stereotype of advanced age as *merely* a time of physical decrepitude and emotional deterioration, and a general disinterest in life. By honoring and highlighting centenarians—who are at the pinnacle of old age—I hope to persuade others to think about the very eldest members of society (those 85 and over) in a more kindly light and recognize their rightful place in society.

One should remember that the author speaks of a minority that will grow exponentially. People over 85 (the group I belong to) will in the next quarter-century double in number, and there is reason to believe that a million or more of the baby boomers will become centenarians. With such prospects, why not rekindle the old sparks now and make society listen to their future needs (which are my generation's already)? A few years ago, Sarah and Elizabeth Delany, both centenarians and black, wrote autobiographical books in which they shared the wisdom they had acquired in their long lives. Like the biblical Job they ask, "Is wisdom with the aged, and understanding with the old?" To which they—and I—would answer, "More often than people think."

The End of the Matter

I spend a fair amount of time these days going to physiotherapy—there always seems to be something amiss, and occasionally I am assaulted by two or more somethings. My *mene tekel* is not yet clearly written on the wall, but when I look hard, the words convey their meaning to me: Your body has been good to you, but—as Dad quipped—every good thing has an end, only a sausage enjoys two ends. I read this popular saying as a warning: Do not be surprised if your reach gets ever shorter, you are no exception from the rule. You have kept the shop open for more hours than most, but evening falls whether you like it or not. Shakespeare had it down pat when he said:

Death, a necessary end,
Will come when it will come.

Everything living has a deadline. I prefer to be prepared for it but do not quite know what to prepare for. So I greet each new day gratefully and whisper the traditional Jewish morning prayer, which features the words *modeh ani*, "I give thanks!" Thanks for being alive and still attuned to the world, ready to face whatever comes within the limits of my power. The analyzer in the Tower of Time said I was drifting in my youth, but I think I am also doing a little steering these days, more than before. My biology is fighting my chronology, and I know which will eventually prevail. Many believe that within thirty years our scientists will have solved the way to manipulate genes into perpetual existence and that the first immortal person has already been born. I will not be around to find out whether the prognostication was accurate. Is it sour grapes to think that life without end will become in time boring without surcease? Maybe it will not be, but I could also be right. I am in Jonathan Swift's corner; the Struldbrugs do not send me. I will, however, agree that the first centenarian marathoner is most probably already alive. Beyond that, I'll stick with the life-and-death cycle humanity has known till now and keep in mind Thomas Jefferson's meditation on the subject:

> There is a ripeness of time for death, regarding others as well as ourselves, when it is reasonable we should drop off, and make room for another growth. When we have lived our generation out, we should not wish to encroach on another.

This is the end of the matter, for even a book has to come to its end. I have talked about a lot of things and hope that readers will find the realities of aging not too daunting—on the contrary, that they will enjoy their own aging to the fullest. Perhaps in their lifetime society will make it easier for them to relish the fruits they harvest. For most of us there is enough privilege to growing old to warrant the price that goes with it. Unfortunately, some of us pay more and even excessively, while others continue to find life a good bargain. If we have the chance to fill our life with meaning we can keep price and privilege in proper balance for quite a while.

I will suggest one small and cost-free intergenerational project to help this desirable development along: Let us no longer use the word "old" as a synonym for "useless." Pillory that usage as flagrantly discriminatory and as politically, socially, and humanly incorrect. We have done it with other terms, and should now benefit a rapidly growing part of our population. The new millennium will be a good time to start. Focus first on the media, and the rest will follow: advertising, schools, and finally private speech. Language is a powerful instrument for change. We who are old deserve to be seen for who we are: individuals who do not want to spend the rest of their days as society's offal, discarded and delegitimated. Most of us still have much to give; rescuing our potential from thoughtless waste and making it available to all will be a common benefit. The young will learn from the exercise, and the old will acquire self-respect. It is a win-win project.

When that happens, the biblical saying cited in chapter 8, presently unpopular, may gain new currency: "Grey hair is a crown of glory." That would herald another "new age."

Acknowledgments

My colleague at Holy Blsossom Temple in Toronto, Rabbi John Moscowitz, was the first to suggest to me that I should share my feelings and perceptions about growing old with a wider audience. It was he also who enlisted the interest of Rabbi Elliot Stevens, in New York, Executive Secretary of the Central Conference of American Rabbis and head of the CCAR Press. The latter's constant encouragement and advice have been invaluable, and especially his fortuitous choice of Roy Doty as illustrator, Susan Lewis as reader and Amy Fass and Debbie Smilow as line editors. Their perceptions as well as the critiques of Dale Panoff, Joanne Rosenschein, Louise Stern, Rabbi Robert Levine, and Gunther Lawrence helped to give this book its current form and direction.

Among the many others who contributed to my understanding the manifold aspects of aging were Natalie Fingerhut, who once again assisted my research with discretion and good humor, Estelle Latchman and Etta Ginsberg McEwan, who directed me to different sources of insight. I am greatly indebted also to many physicians, researchers and academics, among them Leslie Goldenberg, Morris Moskowitch, Gordon Winocur, Heather Palmer, Milton Israel, Jane McAuliffe, Merrijoy Kelner, and Father Dan Donovan.

Elizabeth, my wife of more than sixty years, was always there for me, and so was the Ineffable One whose Presence never failed to enlarge my perspective.

To say "thanks" to all of them is but a small expression of my deepfelt gratitude.

Notes

PRELUDE: WHY WE AGE

Page 2 *Old age is an incurable disease.* Seneca, *Epistolae Ad Lucilium,* 108:29.

Page 2 *Old age is one big sickness.* Joseph ben Hayyim Tzarfati, in the introduction to his book *Yad Yosef.*

Page 2 . . . *Adam and Eve* . . . Gen. 3.

Page 3 . . . *cryonics* . . . The subject showed 3,913 Web sites in the spring of 1998. Some of them already list the costs of particular services.

Page 3 . . . *the complexity of such life systems* . . . Robert W. Vance, *Encyclopaedia Britannica, Macropaedia,* 5:322.

Page 3 . . . *nanatechnology* . . . Which in the spring of 1998 listed no fewer than 5,980 web sites.

Page 3 . . . *some three billion bases. Encyclopaedia Britannica, 1994 Yearbook,* p. 214.

Page 4 *Journalists were quick* . . . Dr. Vuk Stambolic's research results were front-page news in the Toronto *Globe & Mail,* October 2, 1998.

Page 5 *Birds, for instance* . . . Steven N. Austad, *Why We Age* (New York: John Wiley & Sons, 1997), p. 221.

Page 5 *Aging as a consequence* . . . Steven N. Austad, "Aging: An Incredible Voyage." In *The Incredible Human Machine,* ed. and publ. National Geographic Society (Washington, 1998), p. 252.

Page 5 *Mankind cannot afford* . . . .Sherwin B. Nuland, *How We Die: Reflections on Life's Final Chapter* (New York: Knopf, 1994), p. 78 (shortened)

Page 6 . . . *if you are already suffering* . . . James Christie in the Toronto *Globe & Mail,* September 23, 1998, p. S1.

CH. 1: WHEN I BECAME TIRED

Page 9 *Lord God of Hosts* . . . Rudyard Kipling, *Recessional Hymn.*

Page 11 . . . *those serving in the ancient Tabernacle* . . . Num. 8:23–26. They could assist other Levites, but must no longer "labor."

Page 12 . . . *"senior moment"* . . . William Safire ("On Language," *New York Times Magazine,* May 10, 1998) reports that this now popular expression was first recorded by Dick Dougherty, columnist for the *Rochester*

Democrat. He had heard it used in Florida by an older tennis player who occasionally could not remember the score.

Page 13 *Dr. Gordon Winocur* . . . Interview with Dr. Gordon Winocur, November 1998. I also listened to tapes of his lectures, given in the "Open College" program and broadcast by station CJRT (sponsored by Ryerson Polytechnical Institute in Toronto).

CH. 2: OF MARRIAGE . . .

Page 24 . . . *a devastating blow* . . . I have described this trial, including the letter I wrote her when I learned the news, in *Unfinished Business* (Toronto: University of Toronto Press, 1997), pp. 137–138.

Page 24 . . . *destined for each other* . . . See C. Raymond Knee, "Implicit Theories of Relationships," *Journal of Personality and Social Psychology,* 74:2 (1998), p. 361, with citations of many sources. The author deals extensively with what he calls "destiny theorists" and their opposites, "nondestiny theorists."

Page 25 . . . *there are plenty of books* . . . E.g., Judith Briar and Dan Rubenstein, "Sex for the Elderly," in *The Age of Aging, A Reader in Social Gerontology,* ed. Abraham Monk (Buffalo, NY: Prometheus, 1979). Rabbi Abraham L. Feinberg, my predecessor at Holy Blossom, wrote a book entitled *Sex and the Pulpit,* (Toronto: Methuen, 1981) which wags soon called *Sex* in *the Pulpit.*

Page 25 . . . *more for psychological* . . . Michael Sossin, *Love Life, Live Long, Life Begins at 80* (San Jose, Costa Rica: Interidiom, 1992), p. 67, Cited without specifying the Swedish source.

Page 25 . . . *guided by Jacob Reingold* . . . His obituary, which stressed his contributions to America's old, appeared in the *New York Times* on February 5, 1999.

Page 25 . . . *but sex outside these norms* . . . Joseph L. Esposito, *The Obsolete Self: Philosophical Dimensions of Aging* (Berkeley: University of California Press, 1987), p. 133.

Page 28 . . . *I have described her tale* . . . "The Mutti Phenomenon," *More Unfinished Business,* pp. 197–209.

Page 30 . . . *I visited my mother* . . . Mickey Teicher, "My Mother and I: A Daughter's Role in Caring for Her Mother," in *A Heart of Wisdom: Making the Journey from Mid-life Through the Elder Years,* ed. Susan Berrin (Woodstock, Vt.: Jewish Lights, 1997), pp. 162–165.

Page 31 *Ignorance . . .* Friedrich von Schiller, from his poem *Kassandra.* The original reads: *Nur der Irrtum ist das Leben/Und das Wissen ist der Tod* (literally: Only error is life/And knowledge is death).

Page 31 *"I should have been there."* Philip Roth, *Patrimony: A True Story* (New York: Simon and Schuster, 1991), p. 231.

Page 32 *. . . grandparenthood . . .* This is the title of a recent book by Dr. Ruth K. Westheimer and Dr. Steven Kaplan (New York: Routledge, 1998). In Toronto, a new magazine has been launched, called *Grandparents.*

Page 33 *If I should die . . .* Mary Lee Hall, "Turn Again to Life," in *Masterpieces of Religious Literature,* ed. James Dalton Morrison (New York: Harper, 1948), p. 588, #1899.

CH. 3: HANGING IN . . .

Page 35 *What is it . . .* Matthew Arnold, "Growing Old," *Poems* (London: Macmillan, 1878).

Page 37 *They had their day . . .* W. Gunther Plaut, *More Unfinished Business,* pp. 210–218.

Page 41 *I find there are four reasons . . .* Cicero, *Two Essays on Old Age and Friendship,* translated by E. S. Shuckburg (London: Macmillan, 1927), p. 40. Since the essay on aging is quite short I have provided no further page references to quotations derived from it.

Page 42 *. . . Tho' much is taken . . .* Alfred, Lord Tennyson, *Ulysses.*

Page 45 *. . . its encouragement . . . Pirkei Avot* (Chapters of the Fathers) 4:2. The terse quotation is, "The reward of a *mitzvah* is the *mitzvah.*

Page 46 *. . . two men . . . inexplicably communicate . . .* Martin Buber, "Dialogue," in *Between Man and Man,* trans. Ronald Gregor Smith (New York: Macmillan, 1948), pp. 3–4.

Page 46 *"Thank you . . . "* I have not been able to locate this story.

Page 47 *A person becomes "I" . . .* Martin Buber, *Ich und Du* ["I and Thou"], reprinted in his collected *Werke* (Munich: Kösel, 1962) I:27.

CH. 4: THE VIEW FROM THE TOWER

Page 49 *For age is . . .* Henry Wadsworth Longfellow, *Morituri Te Salutamus,* 281–284.

Page 53 [The aged] Sharon R. Kaufman, *The Ageless Self: Sources of Meaning in Late Life* (Madison: University of Wisconsin Press, 1986), p. 7.

Page 56 *Look closely:* . . . Doris Grumbach, *New York Times,* Nov. 1, 1998 (Week in Review, p. 15). She is the author of *The Presence of Absence* (Boston: Beacon Press, 1998).

Page 57 . . . *this sense of acceptance* . . . Colleen L. Johnson and Barbara M. Barer, *Life Beyond 85 Years* (New York: Springer, 1997), pp. 54f., 76f.

Page 58 *To take things* . . . *The Journals of André Gide,* trans. Justin O'Brien, vol. 4, 1939–1945 (New York: Knopf, 1951), p. 280.

CH. 5: NO ONE CALLS ME OLD

Page 62 . . . *the aged are more heterogeneous* . . . Mark A. Edinberg, psychologist, author of *Talking to Your Aging Parents, 1997,* in a private interview. See also *CARPNews,* February 1999. Colleen L. Johnson and Barbara M. Barer, *Life Beyond 85 Years,* call people aged 65–84 the "young old," 85–99 the "old," and centenarians plus the "old old." I gladly admit that I belong to the middle group.

Page 62 *A bristle-cone pine* . . . Al Cole in the *AARP Bulletin,* June 1989; the author gives credit for the above cited information to *Special Report on Health Magazines,* by Whittle Communication, Knoxville, Tenn, 1989, and for the information on the bristle-cone pine to Nicholas Wade, republished from the *New York Times* in the Toronto *Globe and Mail,* April 18, 1998, p. D8.

Page 63 . . . *archaic, obsolete* . . . *Webster's Third New International Dictionary.*

Page 63 *Age 65 marks* . . . *CARPNews,* February 1999.

Page 64 *In hospitals and hospices* . . . Pierre Ambroise-Thomas, "Old age is still life," in *Dolentium Hominum,* IV:10 (1989), p. 47.

Page 65 *I love everything that's old* . . . Oliver Goldsmith, *She Stoops to Conquer,* Act I, scene 1.

Page 65 . . . *the beginning of social extinction* . . . Joseph L. Esposito, *The Obsolete Self,* p. 2.

Page 66 . . . *the biblical Joseph* . . . W. G. Plaut, ed., *The Torah: A Modern Commentary* (New York: UAHC Press, 1981), p. 271.

Page 66 . . . *When you try* . . . Marcus Valerius Martialis, *Epigrams,* III:42.

Page 66 . . . *a deep-seated uneasiness* . . . Robert N. Butler, "Ageism: Another Form of Bigotry," *The Gerontologist* 9:243 (1969).

Page 67 . . . *ageist terms* . . . Frank Nuessel, in the Monograph Series of the Toronto Semiotic Circle, no. 10, 1992, p.15f. A "Dictionary of Ageist Language" is provided on pp. 19–21. ("Semiotic" means "of or relating to semantics.") Also noteworthy is the survey by Lorna Berman and Irina Sobkowska-Ashcroft, "The Old in Language and Literature" in *Language and Communication*, 6:1/2 (1986), pp.139–145.

Page 67 . . . *they become ageist terms* . . . E.g., D. M. Gamse, *Truth About Ageing: Guidelines for Accurate Communications*, published in 1984 by the AARP. Similar texts exist for use of the media; see Frank Nuessel, "Dictionary of Ageist Language," p. 25f.

Page 68 *Some publications* . . . Sara Rimer (*New York Times*, March 11, 1999, p. B 12), quoting from Mary Pipher's (then forthcoming, now published book) *Another Country—the Emotional Terrain of Our Elders* (New York: Putnam, 1999).

Page 68 . . . *infected with ageism* . . . Already in 1969 *The American Heritage Dictionary* warned readers about it.

Page 69 *Grow old along with me* . . . Robert Browning, *Rabbi ben Ezra*.

CH. 6: I SHOULD BE YOUNG, NOT OLD

Page 71 *Age, I do abhor thee* . . . William Shakespeare, *The Passionate Pilgrim*, stanza 12.

Page 72 *Discipline your child* . . . A colloquial rendering of Prov. 19:18; but the Hebrew original is open to other interpretations. Today, many people believe that physical punishment hinders a child's mental and emotional development. The quotation from Butler is found in his *Hudibras*, pt. 2.

Page 74 *Teenagers today* . . . Noel Semple, "Brave new world of teen autonomy," Toronto *Globe & Mail*, July 13, 1998, back page of the first section.

Page 74 *Our children's friends* . . . Judith Rich Harris, *The Nurture Assumption* (New York: Free Press, 1998).

Page 75 Except in advertisments . . . Carolyn Heilbrun, *The Last Gift of Time: Life Beyond Sixty* (New York, Ballantine Books, 1998), p. 159.

Page 78 . . . *and will not do so here* . . . See my *More Unfinished Business*, pp. 7–8.

Page 79 . . . *that I kicked off* . . . "Taking a driver's test at eighty (years, not km/hr)," Nov. 24, 1992.

Page 80 *Maybe now* . . . *The Star-Ledger* (Newark, New Jersey), Oct. 30, 1998, front page.

Page 81 *Old, but not idle* . . . Quoted in the AARP *Bulletin*, December 1998, with a series of other comments from prominent writers and researchers.

CH. 7: PEOPLE LIKE ME ARE CAUSING PROBLEMS

Page 84 *Since 1900* . . . Figures from the U.S. Administration on Aging, "Profile of Older Americans, 1998," published on the internet (www.aoa.dhhs.gov/aoa/stats/profile). Canadian numbers are found at www.statcan.ca/start.

Page 84 *A whole variety of factors* . . . Ursula Maria Lehr (then West German Minister of Health), "Quality of life and longevity: psychosocial correlations," in *Dolentium Hominum,* IV:10 (1989), pp. 72–78.

Page 84 . . . *advice on how to get there* . . . For instance, Lynn Peters Adler, *Centenarians: The Bonus Years* (Sanata Fe, New Mex.: Health Press, 1995). The author is the founder of the Centenarian Awareness Project. See also David Mahoney and Richard Restak, M.D., *The Longevity Strategy: Live to 100 Using the Brain-Body Connection* (New York: John Wiley & Sons, 1998).

Page 84 *Look here* . . . A colloquial rendition of the biblical account of Israel's enslavement and liberation in the middle of the thirteenth century BCE, Ex. 1:9–10.

Page 86 *Highlighting this trend* . . . Catherine D. Fyock and Anne M. Dorton, *UnRetirement: A Career Guide for the Retired* (New York: American Management Association, 1994).

Page 87 . . . *more equitable trends* . . . Toronto *Globe & Mail,* May 29, 1998.

Page 87 . . . *age discrimination is not illegal,* Thomas R. Klassen and C. T. Gillin, Toronto *Globe & Mail,* Sept. 15, 1998.

Page 87 . . . *discharging an older employee* . . . Reported on the Internet by Ethan A. Winning (May 1998): www.ewin.com/articles/age2.html.

Page 87 . . . *yet every year* . . . Reported on the Internet: www.careerbuilder.com/magazine/atwork/apr_age.html (May 1998; the Web site has since obtained a different URL).

Page 90 *Honoring of patients' wishes* . . . Leah K. Glasheen and Susan L. Crowley, "A Family Affair," *AARP Bulletin,* (May 1998), p. 2f.

Page 91 *Some may prefer* . . . Ibid.

Page 91 *Dr. Kervorkian* . . . He was recently convicted of murder in a Michigan court; his appeal is pending at this writing.

Page 92 *I am now* . . . II Sam. 19:32–36.

Page 92 *Remember God* . . . Excerpted from Eccl. 12:1–7.

Page 92 *Last scene of all* . . . William Shakespeare, *As You Like it,* Act 2, scene 7.

Page 92 *What makes old age so sad* . . . Jean Paul Richter, *Titan,* Zyklus 34.

Page 93 . . . *an insult.* Simone de Beauvoir, *La Vieillesse* (Paris: Gallimard, 1970), English ed. *The Coming of Age* (New York: Putnam, 1972).

Page 93 *I have begun this journal,* Mary Sarton, *At Eighty-two.* (New York: Norton, 1996), p. 27. Ms. Sarton died in 1995.

Page 94 *The reality is* . . . Gordon E. Symons, Toronto *Globe and Mail,* April 11, 1991, p. A18.

Page 94 *Age is a relative matter* . . . Pablo Casals, *Joys and Sorrows: His Story as Told to Albert E. Kahn* (New York: Simon and Schuster, 1970), pp. 15 and 17.

Page 95 *The Johns Hopkins Medical Letter,* November 1998.

Page 96 . . . *exaggeration.* The Associated Press had reported that Mark Twain had died in Europe, whereupon the much alive humorist cabled back: "The report of my death was an exaggeration."

Page 96 *Geronotology has been colossally blind.* Harry R. Moody in his Foreword to *Aging and the Religious Dimension,* ed. L. E. Thomas and S. A. Eisenhandler (Westport, CT: Auburn House, 1994), p. x.

Page 96 *The social scientists* . . . Martin E. Marty in *Religion in Aging and Health,* ed. Jeffrey S. Levin (Thousand Oaks, Calif.: Sage, 1994), p. ix.

Page 97 *African-Americans constitute* . . . See L. M. Chatters and R. J. Taylor, "Religious Involvement Among Older African-Americans," ibid., pp. 196–230.

Page 98 *Health After 50.* Write to The Johns Hopkins Medical Institutions, Baltimore, MD 21205.

Page 99 . . . *the new millennium* . . . Using the common, imprecise parlance. Actually, the new millennium begins with the year 2001.

CH. 8: THEN AND NOW, HERE AND THERE

Page 101 *Some 14,000 children* . . . Cornelia Hummel *et al.,* in Mike Featherstone and Andrew Wernick, eds., *Images of Aging: Cultural Representations of Later Life* (London: Routledge, 1995), p. 167.

Page 102 *Koheleth* . . . Eccl. 7:10.

Page 102 *He studied seventy-one tribes* . . . Leo W. Simmons, *The Role of the Aged in Primitive Society* (New Haven: Yale University Press, 1945). Sixteen tribes lived in North America, ten in South America, fourteen in Africa, three in Europe, sixteen in Asia, and twelve in Oceania and Australia.

Page 103 . . . *turned out to the desert or jungle* . . . Examples of such practices are reported in the volume *In the Country of the Old*, Jon Hendricks, ed. (Farmingdale, N.Y.: Baywood, 1980), p. 57. See further below.

Page 104 . . . *an additional difference* . . . On this see Jay Sokolovsky, ed., *The Cultural Context of Aging*, 2nd ed. (Westport, Ct.: Bergin & Garvey, 1997).

Page 104 *Since Western civilization* . . . See Thomas Cahill's *The Gifts of the Jews: How a Tribe of Desert Nomads Changed the Way Everyone Thinks and Feels* (Garden City: Doubleday, 1998). The author elaborates the thesis that the foundations of much of civilization (not just Western) were ideas contributed by the Jews and contained in their sacred literature.

Page 104 *The years of our life* . . . Ps. 90:10. The psalm is ascribed to Moses.

Page 105 *Do not cast me off* . . . Ps. 71:9; the prayerful request is repeated in verse 18. The verse has been made part of the Yom Kippur liturgy. But Abraham Joshua Heschel extracts a different meaning from the text: Do not cast us into old ways of thinking. Keep us youthful and creative, especially when we contemplate our later years.

Page 105 . . . *at a good ripe age* . . . Gen. 25:8

Page 105 . . . *all is futile* . . . Eccl. 12:7–8.

Page 105 *Grey hair is* . . . Prov.16:31. *The glory of young men* . . . Prov. 20:29.

Page 105 . . . *honor father and mother* . . . Ex. 20:12; repeated with variations in Lev. 19:32 and Deut. 5:16.

Page 106 . . . *children with their parents* . . . Malachi 3:24.

Page 106 . . . *subsequent Jewish tradition* . . . A fine collection of materials will be found in Susan Berrin's *A Heart of Wisdom: Making the Jewish Journey from Midlife Through the Elder Years* (Woodstock, Vt.: Jewish Lights, 1997).

Page 106 *At the age of eighteen* . . . Pirkei Avot (Chapters of the Fathers) 5:21. I have rendered the list not in the crisp style of the original but in a somewhat interpretive way. William W. Hallo has called my attention to *Sultan Tepe*, an old Near Eastern text: "40 equals the prime of life/50 equals foreshortened days/60 equals magisterial age/70 equals length of days/80 equals old age/90 equals ripe old age." (*Monographic Journals of the Near East: Assur* 1/4; April 1976).

Page 107 . . . *rise before an aged person* . . . Lev.19:32.

Page 107 . . . *double honor* . . . I Timothy 5:3–19.

Page 107 . . . *you fathers* . . . Ephesians 6:4.

Page 108 *I think my present age . . . Della vita sobria (On the Sober Life)*, cited by Jose Pereira, "A Christian Theology of Aging," in *Aging: Spiritual Perspectives* (Opera Pia International), ed. Francis V. Tiso (Florida: Sunday Publ., 1982), p. 135.

Page 108 *He was one . . .* Ibid., p. 141.

Page 108 *Society's negative image . . .* Catholic Bishops of the United States, "Society and the Aged: A Reconciliation." May 5, 1976,

Page 109 *The value of life . . .* Pope Jean Paul II, address on September 18, 1985, in Vancouver, B.C.; see *Canada: Celebrating Our Faith* (Boston: St. Paul Editions, 1985), pp. 291–292.

Page 109 . . . *the Quranic statement . . .* Quran, The Greeks, XXX:54. See also Hakim Mohammed Said, "Islam and the Health of the Elderly," in *Religion, Aging and Health: A Global Perspective*, ed. William M. Clements (New York & London: The Haworth Press, 1989), pp.27–38. The publication appeared under the auspices of the World Health Organization (WHO) of the United Nations.

Page 110 . . . *of happiness the summit . . .* Sophocles, *Antigone*, cited by Louis Roberts, "Portrayal of the Elderly in Classical Greek and Roman Literature," in *Perceptions of Aging in Literature: A Cross-cultural Study*, ed. Prisca von Dorotka Bagnell and Patricia Spence Soper (New York: Greenwood Press, 1989), p. 19.

Page 110 *He had good reason . . .* Retold by Moses Hadas, *Ancilla to Classical Reading* (New York: Columbia University Press, 1954), p. 84.

Page 111 *The man who has . . .* Quoted in Bagnell and Soper, *Perceptions of Aging,* p. 26.

Page 111 . . . *equally troublesome . . .* Ibid.

Page 111 *Similarly Aristophanes . . .* Bessie Ellen Richardson, *Old Age Among the Ancient Greeks* (reprint: New York: Greenwood Press, 1969), p. 51. The book also brings many examples of aged people found on Greek vase paintings and contains a long list of persons who by Greek terms became very old (pp. 215–222), as well as a painstaking study of average longevity, which the author calculates to have been just short of 30 years.

Page 111 . . . *families that honor their elder members . . .* Joan Weibel-Orlando, "Grandparenting Styles: The Contemporary Indian Experience," in Jay Sokolovsky, *The Cultural Context of Aging.*

Page 111 *In the Dene community* . . . Joan Ryan, *Doing Things the Right Way: Dene Traditional Justice in Lac La Martre* (Calgary: Calgary Univ. Press, 1995).

Page 112 . . . *various perspectives* . . . A useful condensation will be found in Clements, *Religion, Aging and Health: A Global Perspective.*

Page 112 *Among the Burmese* . . . Daw Khin Myo Chit, "Add Life to Years: The Buddhist Way," ibid., pp. 39–67. The article concentrates on Burmese society.

Page 112 *Confucianism and Taoism* . . . Takehiko Okada, "The Teachings of Confucianism on Health and Old Age," ibid., pp. 101–107; for a broad treatment see the article "Confucianism" in the *Encyclopaedia Britannica, Macropaedia,* vol. 4, and "Taoism" in vol. 17. Also see Fumimaso Fukui, "On Perennial Youth and Longevity: A Taoist View on Health of the Elderly," in Clements, *Religion, Aging, and Health,* pp. 119–131.

Page 114 . . . *exhumed and scattered* . . . Robert J. Maxwell, *In the Country of the Old,* p. 57.

Page 115 *From the lives* . . . L. E. Thomas, "The Way of the Religious Renouncer: Power through Nothingness," in *Aging and the Religious Dimension,* ed. L. E. Thomas and S. A. Eisenhandler (Westport, Ct: Auburn House, 1994), p. 62.

Page 116 *Religion is the paradigmatic solution* . . . Mircea Eliade, *The Sacred and the Profane: The Nature of Religion* (New York: Harcourt, Brace, 1959), p. 210.

Page 116 *This has tended to protect* . . . Erdman Palmore, "What can the U.S. learn from Japan about aging?" *The Gerontologist,* 15:64–67.

Page 116 *Public transportation reserves* . . . Virginia Skord, "Withered Blossoms," in Bagnell and Soper, *Perceptions of Aging.*

Page 116 *The religious image of okina* . . . George de Voos, "Apprenticeship and Paternalism," in Ezra F. Fogel, ed., *Modern Japanese Organization and Decision Making* (Tokyo: Charles Tuttle, 1979), p. 57. See also Shukuro Araki, "Quality of Life of the Elderly in Japan," in *Dolentium Hominum,* IV:10 (1989), pp. 90-92.

Page 116 . . . *the Obasute Mountains* . . . Skord, *Withered Blossoms,* pp. 133 ff.

Page 116 *The flower that is youth,,,* Ibid., p. 137.

Page 117 *There is no facility* . . . B. O. Osuntokun, "The Elderly and Quality of Life in Nigeria," in *Dolentium Hominum,* IV:10 (1989), pp. 105–107.

Page 117 *Chinua Achebe, Things Fall Apart* (New York: Astor-Honor, 1959).

Page 117 *Similarly condemned* . . . Mongi ben Hamida, "A Tunisian View of Longevity," *Dolentium Hominum*, IV:10, pp. 108–110.

Page 117 . . . *among the Nambicuara* . . . Lorna Berman and Irina Sobkowska-Ashcroft, "The Old in Language and Literature, *Language and Communication* 6:1/2 (1986), p. 140.

Page 118 *The status of the aged* . . . Donald Cowgill, *Aging and Modernization* (New York: Appleton-Century-Crofts, 1972).

Page 118 *The more traditional and stable* . . . See further Ellen R. and Lowell D. Holmes, *Other Cultures, Elder Years* (Thousand Oaks, Calif.: Sage, 1995).

POSTLUDE: LOOKING AHEAD

Page 119 *Let me not pray* . . . Rabindranath Tagore, "Fruit Gathering," in *Collected Poems and Plays* (New York: Macmillan, 1916).

Page 119 . . . *a famous woman* . . . W. Gunther Plaut, "The Mutti Phenomenon," in *More Unfinished Business*, p. 197.

Page 121 *The more we make advancements* . . . Elisabeth Kübler Ross (New York: Macmillan, 1970), p. 7–8.

Page 122 . . . *bless them one by one* . . . Jacob blessing his children, Gen. 49.

Page 122 . . . *we learn how to live* . . . Mitch Albom, *Tuesdays with Morrie* (New York: Doubleday, 1997), p. 83.

Page 124 *A cautionary rabbinic tale* . . . Talmud, Hagiga 14b.

Page 127 . . . *even the undertaker* . . . While the quip is generally attributed to Mark Twain, he may or may not be its author. (I owe this caution to Rabbi Bernard Baskin, a renowned bibliophile.)

Page 128 . . . *my keen appetite for perpetuity* . . . Jonathan Swift, *Gulliver's Travels*, ch. 10. More on this will be found in Eugene C. Bianchi's *Aging as a Spiritual Journey* (New York: Crossroad, 1982), pp. 140 ff.

Page 128 *A Conference on Aging and Technology* . . . ed. T. Barnea and E. Stern (Jerusalem: JDC—Brookdale Institute of Gerontology and Human Development, 1992). The report on the conference makes for good reading

Page 128 . . . *fruits garnered from the Tree of Time* . . . These have been expanded upon in Albom's *Tuesdays With Morrie*; see also Jimmy Carter's *The Virtues of Aging* (New York: Random House, 1998).

Page 128 *It has long distressed me* . . . Lynn Adler, *Centenarians: the Bonus Years*, p. ix f.

Page 129 *Is wisdom with the aged* . . . Job 12.12.

Page 129 *My mene tekel* . . . Mysterious words that the Book of Daniel in the Bible (5:25–28) reported to have appeared during a feast given by Belshazzar, king of Babylon, that were interpreted as predicting the end of the monarch's reign.

Page 129 . . . *every good thing* . . . It doesn't quite come across in English; the German reads: *"Alles Gute hat ein Ende, nur die Wurst hat zwei."*

Page 129 *Death, a necessary end* . . . William Shakespeare, *Julius Caesar*, Act II, scene 2.

Page 130 *There is a ripeness* . . . Thomas Jefferson, principal author of the United States Constitution, cited by Sherwin B. Nuland, *How We Die: Reflections on Life's Final Chapter*, p. 73.

Page 131 *Grey hair is* . . . Prov. 16:31.